# The Wisdom of Wildflowers

# The Wisdom of
# *Wildflowers*

Heather Robbins

RESOURCE *Publications* • Eugene, Oregon

THE WISDOM OF WILDFLOWERS

Copyright © 2016 Heather Robbins. All rights reserved. Except for brief quotations in critical publications or reviews, no part of this book may be reproduced in any manner without prior written permission from the publisher. Write: Permissions, Wipf and Stock Publishers, 199 W. 8th Ave., Suite 3, Eugene, OR 97401.

Resource Publications
An Imprint of Wipf and Stock Publishers
199 W. 8th Ave., Suite 3
Eugene, OR 97401

www.wipfandstock.com

PAPERBACK ISBN: 978-1-5326-0316-7
HARDCOVER ISBN: 978-1-5326-0318-1
EBOOK ISBN: 978-1-5326-0317-4

Manufactured in the U.S.A.                    OCTOBER 12, 2016

To Kathryn G

For your wisdom, humor and friendship.
You showed me the true meaning of living in grace.

# Contents

*Acknowledgments* | ix
*Introduction* | xi

Prairie Crocus | 1
Shooting Star | 7
Harebell | 11
Forget Me Not | 15
Western Canada Violet | 21
Silvery Lupine | 25
Prairie Rose | 29
Large Yellow Lady's Slipper | 35
Golden Bean | 39
Sticky Geranium | 43
White Dutch Clover | 47
Western Wild Bergamot | 51
Columbine | 57
Smooth Aster | 63
Black-Eyed Susan | 67
Yarrow | 71
Western Red Lily | 75
Gaillardia | 79
Hedge Bindweed | 83

Plains Prickly Pear Cactus | 89
Prairie Coneflower | 93
Velvety Goldenrod | 97
Scarlet Paintbrush | 103
Baby's Breath | 107
Canada Thistle | 111
Penny Cress | 115
Prairie Sage | 121
Goats Beard | 125

# Acknowledgments

"We are all in the gutter, but some of us are looking at the stars."
—Oscar Wilde

Thank you to my family for always showing me the stars.

Special thank you to my editor, Jenny Gates.

# Introduction

I HAVE ALWAYS LOVED being outdoors. In fact my happiest memories are from when I was a child, playing in the backyard, hiking in the foothills, or camping in the mountains. My precious childhood collections comprised of interesting rocks, leaves, and feathers that I found on my many outdoor excursions. And, of course, I picked wildflowers. Lots and lots of wildflowers. My fledgling imagination, with the stories and scenarios I would invent each time I came across a grove of flowers, was barely contained within my tiny body. Wildflowers were an ever-present and integral part of my world of fairies, princesses, and knights in shining armor.

Having lived on a cattle ranch on the Canadian prairies for most of my adult life allowed me to stay close to nature. Today I continue to pick bouquets of wildflowers whenever I can, and nature still sings to me, inspiring my heart and soul to live my best life.

When I see these beautiful flowers now, I am reminded of the many things that have happened in my life and that continue to affect me as I journey through this world. Flowers speak to me of my past, my family, my relationships, and my responsibilities to myself and others. I am inspired to think more positively, feel more deeply, and live life with a grateful, happy heart, just as God intended.

Nature is God's way of helping us calm our thoughts and gently guide us to the answers we seek, answers that are always lying within, but sometimes need gentle nudges to bring them into the light. Wildflowers tell us to pause, take a deep breath, and listen to that inner guidance. They help us pay attention to what our spirit is saying. Tuning into that guidance takes awareness and a willingness to uncover one's true self. Indeed, everything we need to live a beautiful life already lies within us—our innate wisdom, our strength, our grace, and our humanity.

Many of us go through our lives with a deeply rooted sense of not being acceptable or lovable. Unfortunately, most of us received these messages when we were very young, and as we navigated through our lives we found ourselves surrounded by people who unwittingly reinforced those narratives. So it was only natural that we came to believe them and let them define who we are. Little wonder many of us struggle with not feeling valued and respected.

Regardless of where these early messages came from, and how long we have been believing them, it is never too late to change course.

For many of us, the journey through life is not an easy one, but it can still be blessed with the beauty and wonderment of God's love when we approach each day with a grateful, understanding heart. Find the place where your spirit rests, whatever or wherever that is, and begin to listen to your precious inner yearnings.

For me that place is in nature. I completely lay down my defenses when I am out in the fields, and open myself up to hear the songs from my soul. The wildflowers whisper their stories to me, guiding me to my innermost thoughts and feelings. They gently direct me to live well, with peace and grace.

## Prairie Crocus

THE SUN IS HIDING today, entirely concealed behind a gauzy curtain of gray cloud and fog. The horizon fades into the pale mist, creating blurred edges and shrouded forms, as if in a dream that lies just beyond one's grasp. A cold southeast wind whips through the drizzle of rain and sleet, forcefully driving crystalized beads of moisture to the ground. Snowdrifts remain in the shelter of the trees, holding the soil beneath in icy bondage for a little longer.

It is early spring here on the prairies. I make my way carefully along a well-worn, muddy path with the sound of the wind my only companion. The path is slippery and I choose my steps carefully to keep my balance.

On the windswept slope ahead I see the Prairie Crocus— embroidered jewels of softened violet stitched into the muted gold landscape. These brave little blossoms of early spring have broken through the tangle of dead grass and leaves, stretching out and hungrily absorbing the sun's raw March rays. Their pallid stems are fringed with soft silver hairs, offering protection from the crisp, lashing winds. Almond-shaped petals of faded purple curl towards the sky and surround a center of lemon-yellow stamens. As I kneel down to stroke the petals with my finger, I wonder how something so soft and lovely can come from such a cold, dark place.

The exquisite mauve color of the Prairie Crocus perfectly describes the delicate play between the warm rays of the sun and the cool soil of the earth, highlighting how everything in nature exists in a divine balance. I realize how important it is to have balance in our own lives, to be grounded and centered while the bustle of the world spins around us. It is too easy to get caught up in the hectic flush of modern day life, and to easily lose our foothold.

In order to achieve balance in our lives it is important to recognize those elements that pull us off center. How many of us fill our days from dawn to dusk with endless commitments and responsibilities? Our minds race along, switching from one gear to the next, hardly realizing what it is we are even thinking about at any given moment. Our bodies tackle the duties by rote, but our thoughts are somewhere else, usually fussing over what else needs to be done. We get swept up like tender seeds in a swirling wind, looking after everyone else while neglecting our own needs and desires. We convince ourselves there is no time to look after ourselves, and if only we had more time and energy, we could pay attention to what we truly want. But honestly, if we had that extra time, would we not just add more chores to our to-do list?

Tending to this constant stream of activity creates an imbalance in our mind, body, and spirit. Our embattled soul is so completely caught up in the inertia of this unrelenting flurry that our reserves of energy retreat like the sun in a painted twilight sky. This constant depletion of our reserves affects every aspect of our being.

How can we remain healthy and strong when the energy that supports our physical, mental, and emotional health is incessantly stripped away? How long before this imbalance knocks us so hard to the ground that we cannot possibly rise again and are left feeling unsheltered and vulnerable, like naked stones on a windswept slope?

Our spirit aches for a comforting embrace. We hope and pray for some remarkable event to suddenly create more time and space in our hectic lives, thus enabling us to finally look after ourselves. But how long do we think we can wait for that?

The reality is, we should not wait, and we need to pay attention to ourselves right now. We must decide we are worth taking care of today, and look at our life honestly so we can acknowledge those parts of ourselves we are neglecting. Which areas are starved for attention?

Our mind, body, and spirit long for loving sustenance, but we must slow down before we can hear their plea. If we do not take the time and energy to provide this nurturing comfort for ourselves today, it is entirely possible that we will be forced to put in the time and energy later to heal our stressed and diseased bodies, or deal with an emotional breakdown. The problem with waiting until we've "hit the wall" is that by then it may be too late. Do we really need to hit bottom before we learn this valuable lesson?

Many of us are so conditioned to racing around in this marathon called life that we may not even know how to begin the process of finding balance. Fortunately, this is not difficult to do, and only requires the one thing we have been doing since the day we were born—breathing. Breathing is something we do not give much attention to, but it is the first and best step to slowing down and allowing our mind, body, and spirit to mesh into wholeness.

It sounds easy, and it is, but it takes conscious effort on our part. Try it now. Close your eyes. Focus on your breathing. Concentrate on how cool and crisp the air feels in your nose as you inhale. Notice how it changes to warm and moist as you exhale. If your mind wanders, gently redirect your thought back to your breathing. Repeat the exercise several times.

If we can manage even five minutes every day to do this little breathing exercise, our mind will eventually recalibrate into stillness. The habit of maintaining our scattered thoughts, built up from years of frantic activity, will begin to subside, and the mind will create spaces of sweet calm and serenity. It is within these spaces that our authentic self will have the clarity to compose its unique song. Becoming more mindful of our breath not only envelops us in the tranquility of the moment, but also helps to reinforce the connection at the core of who we are—our physical, emotional, and spiritual being. This is the way God intended us to be. The stronger the connection between mind, body, and spirit, the more stable and secure we will feel.

There are many opportunities and techniques we can use to achieve a more balanced and harmonious life, and discovering what they are is something that each individual will come to on their own. Anything that helps us quiet our thoughts—reading, walking in nature, listening to music, sitting quietly by ourselves—will benefit us, help us find balance, and enrich our connection with God.

Each life is as unique and remarkable as spring raindrops, and because no two are alike, finding solutions in creating spaces of calm will be different for each of us. The important factor here is to at least begin the process of nurturing our beautiful being, regardless of how much time we can devote to it right now. And as we learn to care for our mind, body, and spirit, our nimble steps on life's path will become more courageously defined and secure. Life will take on more flavor because we will have the time and energy to savor each hour of each blessed day.

Naturally, the more balanced we are in our lives, the more everyone around us will benefit. And what a wonderful, selfless gift that would be for our loved ones if they can learn from our example and give themselves permission to take care of themselves.

Thank you, brave, soft little Prairie Crocus for showing us the importance of having balance in our lives.

# Shooting Star

SPRING IS WELL UNDERWAY. Baby animals are appearing all over the countryside while their anxious mothers hover nervously nearby. New leaves are sprouting from awakening trees, painting the horizon a brilliant lime green. A light breeze slips silently through the azure sky, caressing my cheek with the softness of a downy feather.

Springing up from the tender loam where I am standing is a Shooting Star, stretching with all its might and resolve towards the glorious heavens. Vivid pink-colored petals lay back from bright-yellow, tube-like stamens. The stem is a delicate pale-green thread, surrounded by several lance-shaped leaves at its base. This little blossom looks so precious as it reaches up into the warm embrace of the sky.

How many times have I made a wish after catching a fleeting glimpse of a shooting star as it blazed across the night sky, and searched my heart for what I most desired at that point in time. I have wished for so many things, dreamed of so many things. And although I cannot say all my dreams and wishes have come true, I still believe it is so very important to continue to have these yearnings, to dream and set goals for the future we desire for ourselves.

Where would we be if we stopped dreaming? What would our world look like? Dreams are not silly, insignificant thoughts to be dismissed when the blinding light of reality descends. They are very important to our overall well-being. I cannot imagine that our species would have evolved as it did if people stopped pursuing their dreams. Sometimes it is even enough to simply have the dreams, and to let our sentimental thoughts slip into a world of fantasy where we set the pace and make the rules. These dreams are fun and nourishing to our soul. They are like mini-vacations of the mind—there to enjoy and bring us pleasure.

However, there are some dreams that do not belong in the fantasy world, and should be brought into the light of day where they can be turned into reality. Of course, this then requires setting goals whereby if the dream is the vision, the goal is the tangible outcome of that vision. If the dream is to be a teacher, then the goal is to get an education degree and land a teaching job. If the dream is to swim alongside a giant tortoise, the goal is to save enough money to take a trip to the Galapagos Islands.

Because turning dreams into reality is not always easy, many will not even attempt to pursue their heartfelt yearnings. Instead, they perceive all the obstacles in the way and give up before they even get started. There are those who are just not up to putting in the time and effort to pursue their dreams, and some will begin, but then lose heart and decide there's no point in continuing.

No one ever said achieving a dream was easy. In fact, most people who are living their dreams today had to go to great lengths to get there, and put in a lot of work, time, and energy before they achieved their goals. Many even had to make tremendous sacrifices. We usually just see the end result of their labors, and then desire that for ourselves. We do not always see and appreciate the long and sometimes arduous journey they had to travel in order to make their dreams a reality.

It can be extremely difficult to muster up the strength to turn the dream of being a teacher into a reality when one is a single parent with a full-time job and a Grade 10 education. But regardless of where we are in life at the moment, in order to turn our dream into a reality we need to first believe we deserve it, and that we have what it takes to achieve it. Once we know this, once we have that belief in ourselves and know that God is ever present to guide us, the next step is researching what it will take to turn that dream into a reality.

What is the first step? What is the first goal that needs to be achieved? When we look at the expanse of time and work that may be necessary to fulfill our dreams, it can be overwhelming. However, by breaking things up into manageable bits and taking one step at a time, with determination and perseverance, we will get there in the end. It is also important to have reasonable expectations about timelines and accomplishments when undertaking this endeavor. But by holding onto the dream and using it as a guiding light, and trusting God is by our side, our spirit will be buoyed by our energy and enthusiasm, keeping us moving forward when we hit those inevitable roadblocks.

It is so important to mark every step, celebrate every achievement regardless of how small or insignificant it may seem, and we must take care to not let any negative thoughts pull us off course. Negative messages are just tiresome transcripts that we have been feeding ourselves for far too long. They have no place in our glorious future and we must not give them any attention. It is also important to surround ourselves with people and resources that will support and encourage us along the way. Negativity from anywhere, whether internal or external, will make the journey that much more difficult.

Imagine what living our dream would feel like. Do we not deserve to have that in our lives? Is that not what God wants for us? And yes, it could take years to reach our goal, but the longer we delay in taking that first step, the longer it will be before our dream is a reality. By actively pursuing our dreams, regardless of how much time or effort we can devote to it at this moment, it enlivens the spirit and makes the hours, days, and even years slip by a little easier.

There is only one difference between the woman who is not living her dream and the one who is. The woman living her dream faced all the demons, jumped through all the hoops, and persevered until she got what and where she wanted. In other words, she went for it, and we can do that, too.

Let us honor our dreams and set goals for our glorious future. Let us take charge and make the necessary decisions to have the life we deserve. And like the Shooting Star tells us, let us aim high and expect the best.

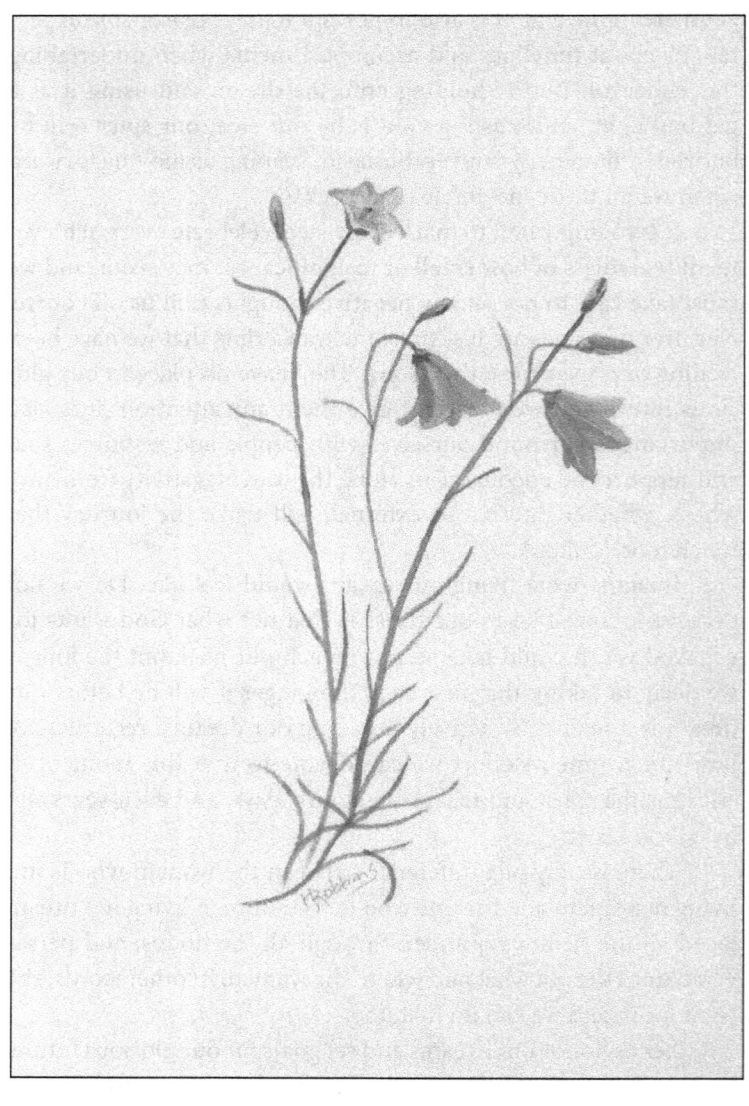

# Harebell

Foamy white clouds drift lazily through a brilliant blue sky, silently slipping their violet shadows over the early summer landscape. The waves of dark and light make the land swell in rolling emerald waves—a shimmering sea of jewels.

Swaying playfully in this ocean of green are dozens of blue-violet Harebells. The whispery soft and delicate bell-shaped blossoms, with their five-pointed edges, look to be made of translucent blue tissue paper. I am certain they would disintegrate if even a drop of rain splashed on their sides. Slender pale-green stems rise from crowns of lance-shaped leaves, holding the blossoms up in the fragrant summer breeze.

The Harebell looks like an elfin hat that a woodland fairy might wear. It captures my gaze and takes me back through the years to when I was a child. I remember trying in vain to catch a glimpse of those elusive sprites that I was certain lived and played among the foliage and trees in the nearby woods. Alas, I never saw one, but I knew in my childhood heart they existed. I just had to be on guard and employ my best sleuthing techniques to seek them out.

I do not remember when I stopped searching, or when my child-like imagination was silenced and I no longer believed in the unbelievable. There is a part of me that misses that state of sweet innocence and wonder, and I realize how important it is to hang onto some part of that eternal child. The part of our spirit that is optimistic, sweet, affectionate, and young at heart. The part that is touched by magic and fantasy.

As children, our dreams and imaginations spilled out from our little hearts and souls, barely contained within our excited earthly bodies. We sprang out of bed each morning, eager to get out and explore the world. There were simply not enough hours in the day to get in all the important discoveries we were trying to make. I know I would have found those fairies with the Harebell hats had it not been for my 8:00 p.m. bedtime! But as we grew older most of us lost that youthful enthusiasm. We became all too aware and concerned about our image, and what other people thought of us. We put aside what we perceived as childish nonsense, and strove, en masse, towards our duties and responsibilities.

Our lives are not always as fun as they used to be. We laugh less, we explore less, and because we allowed the dark, heavy burdens of our adult world to weigh us down, we grew old. And we did that without even realizing we were losing a very special quality.

Let us reawaken that child-like enthusiasm, and rekindle our imaginations that have long been silenced by our terribly important, grown-up lives. Be kind. Be curious. Get excited about things. Learn something new. Shower unconditional affection on those we love, not because we expect anything in return, but just because we can. Be generous with our smiles and laughter. Show the world our warmth and tenderness. Our world will be a much better place if we all allowed our inner child its rightful expression. Begin again to wonder about the mysteries in life. We have not discovered all its secrets.

I am certain the Harebell knows the whereabouts of those fairies. Let us all go out there and see if we can find them.

# Forget-Me-Not

TAKE A MOMENT TO close your eyes and imagine the purest shade of blue you can. A hue that is crisp, soft, and wonderfully simple. I am certain the color of the Forget-Me-Not is exactly the shade of blue you have in mind.

These plants grow abundantly in the foothills. Delicate sprays of miniature blue flowers stand twelve to eighteen inches high on pale-green stems. They have the cutest blossoms one could ever imagine, with tiny pale-yellow discs surrounded by five perfect little blue petals. The soft hue is so pure and fresh, it greets the eye like a soothing breeze on a hot summer's day.

The name of the Forget-Me-Not speaks to the lesson this beautiful blossom has in store. And although poets in the past wrote of it as a token of affection between lovers, we can look at it as a reminder to never forget our past, and to understand and recognize where we came from.

Our personal history is the rich soil in which our roots are embedded, and regardless of what lies buried there, it is the ground from which we came. How we grow today is our choice, but looking back can provide tremendous insights into the path we have chosen for ourselves. Peering into the past lifts a veil, allowing us to discover the intricacies of our unique personality. And not only can we excavate the depths of our own persona, but we can also discover the richness of our family's history.

Looking into that history can reveal wonderful and exciting discoveries about the time spent with family and loved ones. But for those who had difficult past experiences in their lives, it can be a very painful exercise. Nevertheless, in order to move forward, we must sometimes look at where we've been.

What circumstances influenced our decisions? What did we have control over, and what did we not? Which family behaviors and traditions do we want to carry forth into our own lives and pass onto future generations? Which behaviors and traditions do we want to see end? Were we lifted up and supported, or did words and actions from our loved ones tear us down? What made us stronger? What continues to eat away at us and rob us of our power today?

Rooting through our past can help dislodge deeply held negative thoughts and feelings, which we can then confront and deal with. Fortunately, for those who find doing any of this too overwhelming on their own, there are many counseling resources available in communities and online to help guide them through.

If it is not possible to look back at our past with loving smiles and a happy heart, then perhaps we can look back with some understanding. When we delve even further into our family's story and see what the childhoods of our parents or caregivers were like, it may help us understand what shaped their behavior and made them into the people they are.

Did they have loving influences in their early years? Was there a lot of pain and anguish? Did their little spirits retreat from an unrelenting stream of abuse and mistreatment? What did their lessons in love look like?

It can be very difficult to shower love and affection on someone when your own wellspring of emotion was never filled or replenished. We learned how to express love and kindness from those who expressed love and kindness towards us, but if our caregivers were never shown how to do that, how could they possibly have loved us the way we needed them to?

The more we understand how and why our family members behaved as they did, the clearer the path towards forgiveness. We must remember, however, forgiveness does not mean condoning behavior. It simply means we understand where that behavior comes from, and we make the decision to no longer let it influence us.

When we are flooded with the memories from past negative experiences, it is important to allow ourselves to completely feel the emotion of it. Conjuring up painful memories is a very uncomfortable process, but they are just memories, and the actions that precipitated those feelings are no longer present. We are in control now and we are safe. Once we allow ourselves to feel the pain, then we can release it. We can cry it out, scream it out, pray it out, or just close our eyes and imagine the hurt draining out of our bodies with each exhaled breath. And each time the pain rises up, we can acknowledge it, feel it, and release it. If we fight the emotions and try to block them out, all we are doing is holding them tighter to us. We need to call them out and release them.

This is an exercise that will probably need to be repeated again and again, but each time we do it, each time we allow ourselves to feel the pain associated with the memory, and then let it go, the pain will become less and less until the day comes when we are no longer held captive by it.

It can be a bit like watching a scary movie. The first time we watch the film our reactions are very strong. However, if we watch the movie again and again, our reactions become less pronounced. If we continue to watch the film, we will get to a point where the scary parts no longer shake us to the core.

It is the same with unpleasant memories that have created anguish in our heart. Each time we allow ourselves to feel the pain, and each time we acknowledge what happened in the past, we become less captive by it. We realize that now we are in the driver's seat, that we are in control. We are safe to feel the emotion, and we can work on setting ourselves free.

When we are aware of our family's history and dynamic, we can make better, more informed choices for our own lives, as well as for the lives of those who come after us. We cannot change our past, and it will always be a part of us. But we do not have to continue to carry the heavy chains that were forged by pain and anger, and passed down through the generations. We can be the change that puts our family's story on a smoother, gentler track. Remember, we will be part of the past that future generations will look back on, so what do we want them to see? Our strength, our grace, and our humanity, or that we continued to carry pain and heartache, and pass it onto the next generation?

Just the fact some of us are alive today is an incredible testament to our family's will to survive. The lives of our ancestors were much different than what we are experiencing today. Their time on earth was probably very difficult. They would have made tremendous sacrifices, endured back-breaking work, and faced painful and difficult choices. Whatever their circumstances, a tenacious, driving spirit would have carried them through, and we have inherited that spirit, that incredible strength that helped our ancestors through wars, famines, depressions, and loss.

Regardless of what other attributes they carried with them, our ancestors were survivors, and so are we. There will always be days when we feel overwhelmed and vulnerable, but if we have faith that our family's strength of spirit beats strong and true within us, and that God's divine love is ever present, that will be the legacy we carry into the future.

Our history, like the delicate Forget-Me-Not tells us, is full of precious stories and interesting people. We are all sewn into the embroidered lace of our family's tale. Let's make an effort to understand our past, embrace our present, and make our lives a beautiful and inspiring chapter for future generations to discover.

# Western Canada Violet

The aspen grove is quiet and still this morning. Only the occasional trill from the Savannah Sparrows filters through the calm. I know I am not entirely alone in this beautiful place.

The air is redolent from the fertile loam, inviting my lungs to drink in the delightfully rich breath of nature. On the matted forest floor I find a Western Canada Violet poking its timid little head out from a crowd of heart-shaped leaves. Five creamy-white petals cling together at a center point, with dark veins radiating subtle bursts of tawny brown and gray from the middle. This violet has chosen a very tranquil and secluded place to make its home. It is this seclusion that enables it to survive.

Sweet, sweet solitude. How many of us dream of periods of quiet calmness in which to rest our frantic minds and bodies? Or of a time when life slows down for an hour so we can get our thoughts in order? Even if we achieve that, some of us are afraid to be alone for very long because that might mean we are not wanted, that we are ignored by the world, that we have been shut out. No one wants to be left out or forgotten, and while we yearn for some alone time, many of us also resist the urge to be on our own for very long.

We have always been social beings. Our ancestors traveled in packs because traveling alone meant they were vulnerable to attack from another tribe or perhaps an animal. They knew there was safety in numbers. Today we carry that primordial instinct to remain with the group, and even though we do not need to fear a lion attack when we are on our own, many of us are still uncomfortable with solitude. We have now replaced the lions with the societal expectations of remaining constantly connected to other people.

In this day and age it is so easy to avoid solitude. We are perpetually connected to the world through our cell phones, social media, and the television remote. What will people say if we choose to be on our own instead of caught up in the flush of society? What will people think if we decide not to "do lunch" or volunteer for a half dozen charities? How will it look if we sit by ourselves in the park? No one wants to be branded a "loner," so we fill our lives with activities and noises to dispel all thoughts of aloneness. We want to show the world that we are popular and wanted. We want to convince ourselves of the same.

And yet, spending time quietly on our own is so important and necessary for our well-being. Solitude is not the same as being lonely. Loneliness happens when we are scattered and disconnected from ourselves and our Creator. By comparison, solitude paves the way for our mind, body, and spirit to unite and recharge, and allows us to connect to God and listen to his subtle guidance. We need to focus inward on who we are, and begin to reintroduce and reconnect all the parts of our being. Solitude helps to make us complete and whole.

Being alone gives us the time and space needed to process the events of our lives. It allows us to reflect on how we are doing, what we are thinking, how we are feeling, and where we want to go in life. As we journey along life's path, there are things that take time to reveal themselves to us, but if we do not slow down and pay attention to those directions, we may miss them completely. When we are quiet, we can more easily hear the inspired song that our heart and soul are singing. We cannot hear these important messages when we are standing in a crowded room with our attention being pulled to and fro, or frantically scrolling through social media so we will not miss anything.

Solitude is necessary for our physical, mental, and emotional health, so we should not be concerned what other people think or say about our occasional seclusions. When we take the time to recharge our batteries, we will be stronger because of it.

Solitude is the opportunity for us to really know and understand the magnificent woman we see every day in the mirror. We will discover our strengths and weaknesses, understand what we need to work on, and know what we can let go. Clarity comes from being quiet and still. Our alone time will help liberate all mental and physical stresses, and make us less vulnerable in the world. Being confident, calm, and having self-awareness gives us a strength that no lion would dare challenge.

As the story of the Western Canada Violet whispers to us, let's make some time in our lives for solitude.

# Silvery Lupine

It rained last night, not a lot, just one of those showers that washes the dust off everything and leaves the air clean and cool. I am out for a quick walk this morning. Everything seems renewed and energized after the rain, and each breath I take is a cool, healing embrace of my spirit. Mother Nature has again performed one of her many duties and made everything right with the world.

My boots glisten like polished marble as they brush against the still damp grass. I continue down the path until I come to a steep precipice. The earth has slowly eroded away, leaving a bank of tanned clay and jagged rock.

At the bottom of the bank stand a dozen or so Silvery Lupines. They look so regal in their royal colors. A cluster of purplish-blue blossoms cling dutifully to the pale-brown stem, decreasing in size as they approach the top. Daisy-like, greyish-green leaflets spring from the bottom of the stem, as if they are ladies-in-waiting ready to serve.

This flower not only reminds me of the tall, outrageous hairstyles that royal women like Marie Antoinette used to wear in seventeenth-century France, but also how those women, including our own Queen Elizabeth II, epitomize the words duty and responsibility.

One of the least inspiring words in our vocabulary, duty is something that most women know all too well. And just like our current Queen, we are all immersed in duties and responsibilities of one sort or another. As much as most of us would like to wake up one morning and live a carefree existence, the cold hard fact is that we all have duties and responsibilities to look after, and we cannot ignore or walk away from them. How are we tending to those duties and responsibilities? And how do we look after them without sacrificing our health and well-being in the process?

It is so easy for us to fall into the "habit" of looking after everyone else first and putting ourselves last. That is something most of us unconsciously do. We perform juggling acts every day to stay on top of all our duties and responsibilities. When we are strong and healthy, juggling is a breeze, but when we are stressed and weak, we start to drop the balls. It can be difficult to remain strong, healthy, calm, and composed in our lives while the shifting, prairie winds of unrelenting duties continue to swirl around us. The lesson of the Silvery Lupine is that our first duty is to look after ourselves.

God made women to be the nurturers of life, and as soon as we entered adulthood, most of us found ourselves in nurturing and caregiving roles. We have become very important to a number of people, whether it is family, colleagues, employers, friends, or volunteer organizations. They count on us every day to perform our duties, and most of the time we do not disappoint. But when we are tired and have spread ourselves too thin, everything connected to us can pay the price.

In order for people to lean on us for support, we must be well-anchored with very deep roots. Roots that hold us so securely to the ground that nothing will knock us off course. But these roots will only sprout and grow strong when they are nourished and tended to. We can provide that nourishment by looking after ourselves, and tending to our own self-esteem and self-worth. First and foremost, our duty is to develop and nurture those thoughts and feelings within us because our roots will only grow stronger when we take care of ourselves.

Each time we treat ourselves gently and with love, we add precious nutrients to the soil in which we grow. We deserve to be treated with kindness and respect, not just from the outside world, but from our inner world as well. We need to continually reinforce the belief that we are just as important as everyone else. The more we give to ourselves, the more we are able to give to others. The stronger we are, the better we are able to look after others. This is why it is so important to understand ourselves completely, and to know how much we can give, and when we need to pull back and say "no." We cannot perform our duties with a half-charged battery.

We love and cherish our families and friends. We want to help them realize their potential and be the best they can be. They deserve the best we have to offer, but first and foremost, we deserve that for ourselves.

As we continue to look after the long list of people and things in our lives by embracing our duties and responsibilities, let us remember to put ourselves at the top of that list. And like the Silvery Lupine tells us, let us hold our heads up like the queens we are all meant to be as we proudly and confidently take care of our duties.

# Prairie Rose

Raindrops pepper the windshield as I drive along a soggy gravel road. The sky is a muted blue gray, giving the landscape a deep earthy glow. Flanking the road is a soft flush of pale pink, an almost dream-like vista as I look through the wet windows of my car. I stop, pull my coat tightly around me, and step out into the cool, damp country air.

I walk to the side of the road, the gravel crunching and squishing under my boots, and am greeted by hundreds of pale-pink Prairie Rose bushes. They stretch out along the edge of the road like an embroidered piece of rose-colored lace. The tiny thorns adorning the stems prevent me from picking any of the blossoms, though I am tempted to endure the pain just to possess this prairie beauty with its delicious rose scent. Five heart-shaped petals in varying shades of pink surround a pale-yellow center. The rain has made silvery-blue polka dots on the soft blossoms, and gives the sharp-edged oval leaves a glorious green sheen.

For centuries, people have composed songs and poems connecting the Prairie Rose to romance, which is why we often equate the rose with the affection we have for our true love, pure and unfaltering. But what if the lesson of the rose is to develop a pure and unfaltering love for ourselves, just as God loves us? What if we are meant to be our own one true love, the person we are going to spend the rest of our lives with?

For most of us, loving ourselves, or even just being acceptable to ourselves, proves to be such a challenge. We have no trouble loving those who are close to us—our children, family, friends, and partners—but when it comes to having that compassion, nurturance, and kindness for ourselves, most of us struggle. Why is that? Why is it that when we look in the mirror we only see our flaws, faults, and regrets? Why is it so difficult to see our own beauty, goodness, and value?

We loved ourselves when we were very young and there was absolutely no question that we were wonderful, but as we grew older and matured, we traded that innocent childhood narrative for one that was self-critical and negative. Putting ourselves down became a firmly entrenched habit that now shadows our days with dark, heavy storm clouds. Our beautiful spirit was never meant to live beneath this oppressive fog, shrouding ourselves behind veils of negativity. How can we possibly live the magnificent life we were meant to when we repeatedly pull ourselves down? This is not how God sees us, and this is not what he wants for us.

As with all habits, critical self-thinking can be changed, and we can do that by recognizing what it is we believe about ourselves right now. Do we believe we are beautiful? Do we believe we are intelligent? Do we believe we are valuable? If not, why not? Is there something about us we want to change? What about the things we can't change? Do we continue to go through life beating ourselves up about those things?

There will always be things we cannot do anything about, but we can change how we think about them. There is nothing wrong with our beautiful being, our intelligence, or our value; it is our thoughts that are misdirected. Once we recognize and isolate these negative thoughts, we can work at consciously changing them to ones that are gentle and kind. We must challenge the negative thoughts every time they come up. There is no place for them in our wonderful life.

How many of us are consumed by regret for some past behavior? How many of us continually berate ourselves for something we did or said? We cannot change the past, but we can try to understand what precipitated the regretful event, and learn from it.

As human beings, we are going to make mistakes, but when we make these occasional missteps on our journey through life, it is important that we learn from them, forgive ourselves, and then let them go. Yes, we probably did the best we could with the knowledge and understanding we had at the time. And yes, we have more wisdom now, and if we'd had that wisdom before, things might have turned out differently. But we cannot judge our past by the standards or the knowledge we have in the present.

Instead, if we can put these regretful past events into context, then we can see them as opportunities to evolve and grow. God sees our mistakes and forgives us for them, so it is important that we make the time to work on forgiving ourselves as well.

We cannot control everything in our lives, and we cannot change the past, but we can control how and what we think. And since thinking directly influences our feelings and behavior, then if we want to feel better, we need to think better. We need to think of ourselves as beautiful, intelligent, and worthy.

If we experience any negative thought, we can simply acknowledge it, allow ourselves to feel the emotion connected to it, and rephrase that message in a more positive way. This exercise will need to be repeated many times, but each time we do, we strengthen the ties of our loving thoughts to our heart and soul. When we are unburdened by negativity, our beautiful being is reawakened to the wonderful possibilities that God has waiting for us.

In addition to thinking more positively about ourselves, it is also imperative that we treat ourselves in a more loving way. We must give kindness and nurturance to ourselves the same way we do to our loved ones. What actions can we take to love ourselves today? What can we do to reinforce the belief that we are valuable and worthy?

Loving ourselves is the cornerstone to living a beautiful life. When we love ourselves as God does, everything else in our world will improve. We will feel good, we will have stronger relationships, we will be healthier, and we will make better decisions. The more people there are who truly love and accept themselves, the better off our entire world will be.

Like the Prairie Roses that have inspired writers and singers for centuries, let us compose beautiful, loving thoughts for ourselves, and celebrate the wonderful gifts we bring to this world.

# Large Yellow Lady's Slipper

Since moving to the prairies, I have been spellbound by the variety of wildflowers that exist here. But none have brought me as much joy and awe as the day I stumbled upon a Large Yellow Lady's Slipper.

The exquisite June sun flooded the landscape with a swathe of soft rays, while the breeze caressed the lush vegetation with rhythmic strokes. The ditch that runs along the hayfield was laden with a wide range of succulent grasses, and standing proudly among the glorious blades stood the Large Yellow Lady's Slipper. Its immense lemon-yellow flower bobbed ever so slightly in the redolent air as it clung to a pale, smooth stem. Light-green leaves, looking like thick blades of a handsome knight's sword, sprouted along the length of the plant. The Large Yellow Lady's Slipper is a very rare flower, and it is unlawful to pick one. Finding them is like finding gold, and it always makes my day better.

The Large Yellow Lady's Slipper reminds me of the story of Cinderella, and how the prince searched the countryside in order to do the honorable thing and return a glass slipper to its rightful owner. As a result, he found his one true love. Even though this story is only a fairytale, I know there are a lot of Prince Charmings out there who try every day to do the right and honorable thing.

I believe that most men have integrity, are respectable, honest, and absolutely love their families. More often than not, however, it seems women are pitted against men in our society—the "Battle of the Sexes," so to speak. When a group of women get together, the conversation invariably drifts towards the men in our lives, and how they make us crazy. It is very easy to fall into the trap of ragging on our male partners.

I am certain that since the dawn of human kind, women have been talking and complaining about their men, just as I'm sure men have been grumbling about us, and that is not likely to change any time soon. What we must remain aware of though is that most of the men on this planet are inherently good, and want to do the right thing. Some may be a little rough around the edges, but they truly do have hearts of gold.

Men have their own challenges to face in society. There is great pressure on them to be strong and independent, and not let their emotions rule their days. There is an unspoken pressure on them to never appear unsure of themselves or vulnerable and scared. A lot of us want to believe our male partners are strong and brave, someone who will be there for us to lean on when we are on shaky ground. But we forget that at times men also feel vulnerable and scared, and they need to hear loving and encouraging words from us. They need to hear they are doing a good job, we appreciate their efforts, and we love who they are. When we speak to the king in the man, the king will reveal himself to us.

Whether or not men and women will ever see eye to eye about everything and live in complete harmony remains to be seen. But remember that most men are doing the best they can. They care about their families, work hard, and try to make this world a better place. A woman can bear a lot if she has a good man beside her. And remember that we are not always easy to live with either.

Like the Large Yellow Lady's Slipper tells us, love and respect the Prince Charmings in our lives, for they truly are worth their weight in gold.

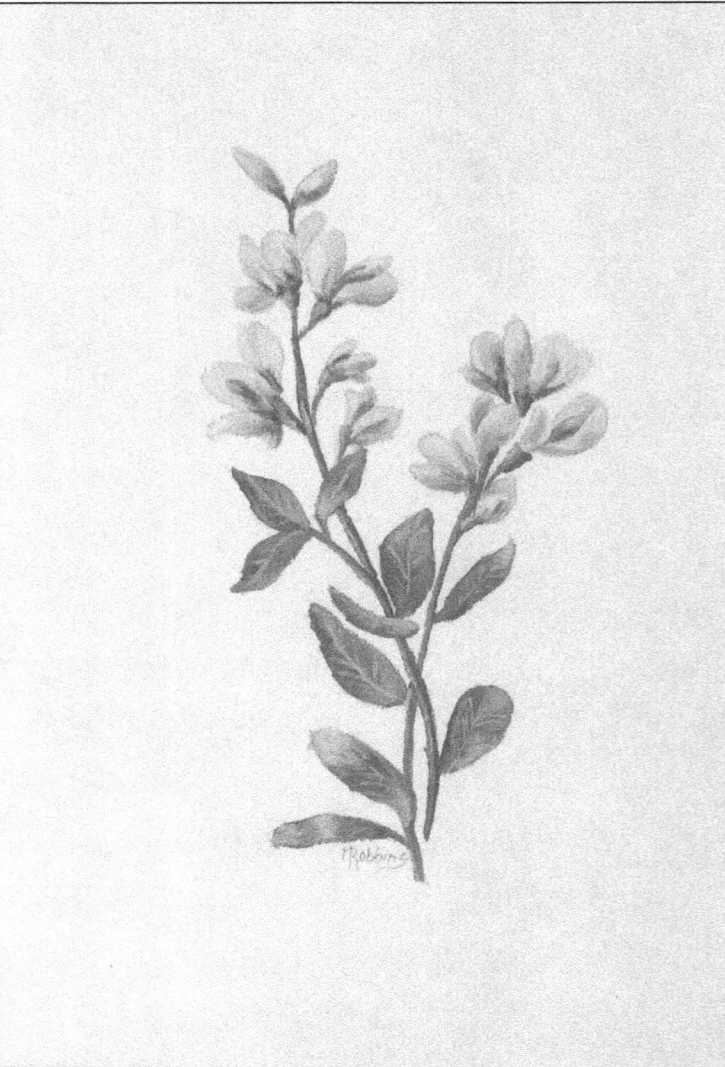

# Golden Bean

A PAIR OF MALLARD ducks lift off from the beaver pond and fly up into the bracing cobalt sky. They quack noisily at me, scolding my indifference at disturbing their peaceful nesting site. I stand quietly at the edge of the pond and watch them disappear beyond a grove of shivering aspen poplars. But my eyes are soon drawn to the other side of the pond where an explosion of bright yellow meets my gaze.

I make my way across a shallow part of the water, and suddenly find myself embraced by a community of Golden Beans. They put on such a display of color that I soon forget about the ducks I have just offended.

The plants stand together, spilling their bright sun-kissed colors over the entire landscape. Each flower consists of a cluster of crescent-shaped blossoms that appear to be made of raw yellow silk. Leaves are long, pale-green ovals that linger languidly on the sides of robust stems. The effect of all these Golden Beans together is spectacular. Their community is rich because of all who inhabit there.

As important as it is to be unique, to stay true to ourselves, and to have alone time, it is also important to maintain a healthy social life. As social creatures, we are compelled to have a relationship with our fellow human beings. Maintaining a connection with others while not being consumed by all the hustle and bustle of life, requires that we walk a delicate and sometimes tricky path. We must decide, without compromising our individuality, what level of interaction will enable us to contribute to society.

Regardless of the level of participation we are willing to contribute, the important thing is to maintain a connection so we can help enrich our community.

Volunteering is a great way to meet our social needs and make a valuable contribution to the place we call home. Society as we know it would not exist if it were not for those who contribute their time and energy free of charge to help others. There simply is not enough money out there to pay every single person for every single deed. Volunteering is essential to keeping many important projects going. Non-profit organizations rely heavily on volunteers to help support those less fortunate, clean up and beautify our spaces, and bring attention to worthy causes both at home and around the world.

When we volunteer our time to make our community better, the rewards returned to us are immeasurable, partly because of what it does to our inner world. By opening our hearts to a cause and sharing freely of our gifts, a wonderful sense of meaning and benevolence sweeps over us. When we are kind and show care and compassion to others, that kindness is returned in unimaginable ways.

People who volunteer show us the true heart of humanity. They show us the essence of God. It is this heart and understanding that has allowed our species to evolve as it has. We have come this far because people have cooperated and helped each other. Many individuals in the world give of themselves for no other reason than to make things better for everyone else. When we follow the example of these extraordinary people, we allow our own bright spirit to shine, spilling light and beauty over everything we touch. Who doesn't feel good after genuinely helping someone or making a much-needed contribution?

Volunteering also gives us opportunities to interact and learn from others. In this day and age, our communities consist of many diverse and vibrant cultures and races. We are greeted with a variety of different religions, customs, and celebrations that are wonderfully unique and interesting, all with incredible histories and stories. Our society is tremendously rich and diverse, and by broadening our societal horizons, we can better understand and appreciate all the groups and qualities that make up our community. Volunteering can help bring us closer to those groups, and develop a better understanding of their richness. The more we understand each other, the less we will fear the unknown, and the more we will ensure a peaceful and harmonious coexistence.

Contributing to our community does not mean we have to join an established organization. We can all do our bit by simply keeping our immediate surroundings clean, picking up any garbage lying around, or offering to shovel snow from an elderly neighbor's sidewalk. We can donate money to causes we deem worthy, or buy a grocery item for the food bank when we do our own shopping. There are so many little things that we can do to make our community shine so much brighter.

Being present and involved with our community enriches many lives, but mostly it nourishes our own heart and soul. It makes us feel good, and at the end of the day, how we feel about ourselves and what we have accomplished is really what makes for a happy life.

Listen to the tale of the Golden Beans. When we all do our bit and work together, kindness and beauty spills over our landscape, making our world a much better place to live.

## Sticky Geranium

I REMEMBER GOING TO the carnival as a child. The fairgrounds were filled with crowds of happy people, soaring laughter, bright glittering lights, and a myriad of tinkering bells and whistles. The shouts of the carnival vendors collided in a chorus of merriment throughout the jubilant air, trying to entice people to play their jaunty games. Cheerful squeals and screams sprang from those on the various rides, and wonderful aromas of corndogs and French fries wafted on perfumed winds from the kiosks. Of course, a day at the carnival was never complete without a must-have bag of cotton candy, and I thought nothing of partaking of that sweet, sticky indulgence.

The Sticky Geranium reminds me of cotton candy because it looks equally decadent and delightfully sweet. This delicious pink beauty is usually found on open, grassy hillsides, with its blossom of five rounded petals merrily curling ever so slightly at the edge, and dark pink veins radiating from its enchanting center. Each blossom sits on top of a pale, sticky stalk that holds the Sticky Geranium upright as it silently calls to passersby to stop and drink in its beauty. What delightful lesson can this engaging wildflower teach us?

In this day and age where one is tied to routines, consumed by schedules, and bombarded with constant reminders to eat healthy and exercise, we must be reminded that once in a while a little self-indulgence can be a wonderful remedy for a tired soul. Sometimes a girl just needs a piece of cake! She needs to occasionally indulge in something that serves no other purpose than pure, personal enjoyment. Think of these frolicsome activities as a kind of nourishment that bathes the flagging spirit with vitality and light.

When we were children, we unintentionally celebrated the miracle of our life and our place in it. We did not think twice about our entitlements and what we deserved. If we wanted ice cream for breakfast, we thought nothing of asking for it. We probably did not get it, but there was a part of our little being that knew we should have it.

As we grew older, the ebb and flow of our lives carried us into whirlwinds of obligations and responsibilities, washing away our inner reserves of strength and self-confidence. The waves of worry and expectation lapped at our vulnerable spirit, and wore down our precious reserves of vitality into slurries of tired sand. Our spirit vanished beneath the relentless pounding of these unremitting commitments. There was no time to take care of ourselves, and no energy to fill our depleted wellsprings of self-worth. Obligations and responsibilities are not things we can turn our backs on. They are stamped into the fabric of our daily lives and must be attended to. We simply cannot stop taking care of our family, working in or outside of the home, or fulfilling our community and social obligations. And that is exactly why it is so important to brighten our lives with the occasional self-indulgence, or allow little shimmering points of sweet, gentle light to season our days.

Why wait for a special occasion to indulge? Why only on birthdays, anniversaries, and holidays? Isn't it also important to celebrate our life and accomplishments for other reasons throughout the year? What about taking a little extra time here and there to treat ourselves to something delightful, whether it's a mini-vacation, an afternoon at the spa, or the simple act of enjoying a specialty coffee on a break from work? Think of such indulgences as investments in our soul, and a reward for a job well done and a life well lived.

Remember the story of the Sticky Geranium and occasionally treat yourself to something wonderfully rich, sweet, and well deserved.

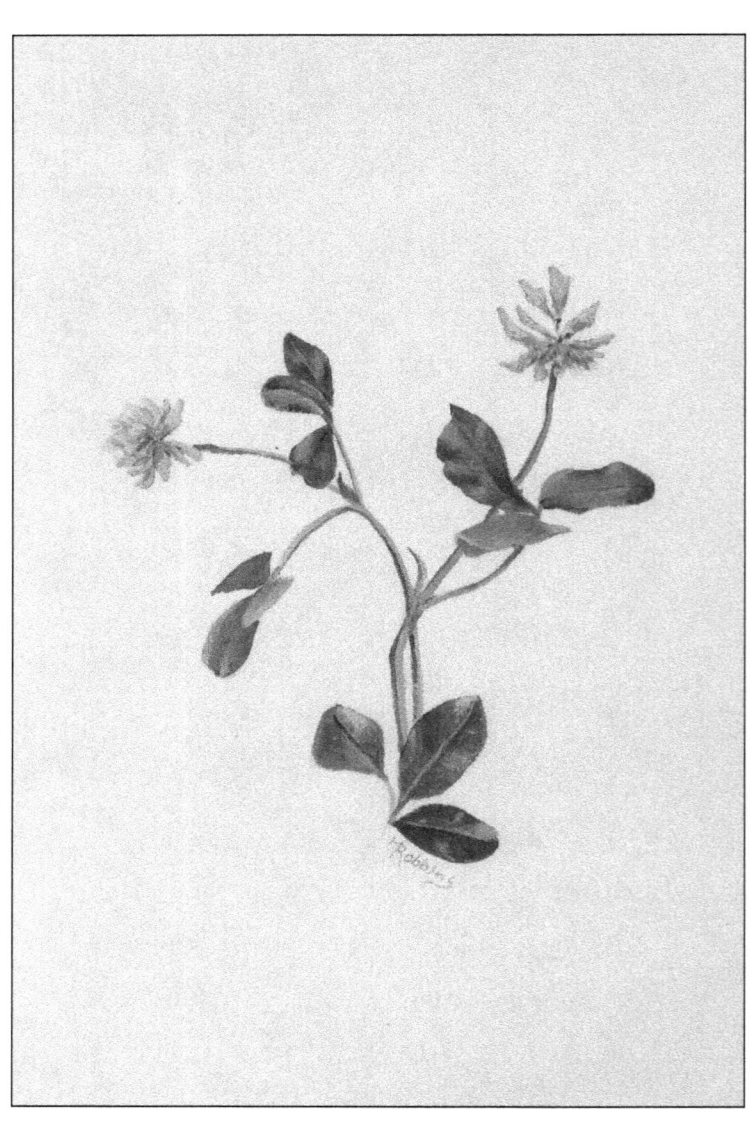

# White Dutch Clover

The summer day throbs with color, movement, and sound, swirling all the senses together in a harmonious symphony. Birds in the trees flit from branch to branch, chirping and singing to their hearts' content. Wildflowers and grasses respond in kind by displaying a rainbow of color under the cheery prairie sun.

Not to be outdone, the White Dutch Clover shines brilliantly, with its rounded mound of stems and leaves sprinkled with spots of succulent ivory. From a distance, the blossoms resemble cream-colored Chinese paper lanterns, luminous against a backdrop of rich, green foliage.

I pluck a floret from its sprawling, slender stem, and slowly twirl it between my thumb and forefinger. Each blossom is made up of ten to twenty bird-shaped flowers, all clinging securely to a small brown pod. A trio of oval leaflets sprouting along each stem create a bower of brilliant green.

This flower always takes me back to when I was a little girl running and playing in the limitless expanse of my childhood imagination. I saw each of the petite buds as a miniature bird, with a tiny pale-green beak, and delicate pearly wings stretched out behind. I spent many hours playing with these lovely little "birds," flying all around the yard, making wonderful discoveries, and having thrilling adventures.

Today, the White Dutch Clover not only speaks to me of birds, but also of all the other animals with whom we share this planet. Its lesson is to celebrate the existence and blessed companionship that our animal friends can provide, and to respect them and be grateful for their presence in our lives.

God has provided a world that is rich with many delightful and interesting animals. They provide us with food, aide us in transportation and labor, and give us companionship. Our lives are so intertwined with and enriched by the presence of animals. Listen to the birds sing in the early morning. The symphony of birdsong is a sound sweeter than anything I have ever known. Or the haunting cry of the coyote, as its plaintive notes weave their melody through a twilight sky. Watch as wild geese glide upon azure winds while making their annual migration to and from their nesting grounds. These are but a few gifts that come from the untamed beating heart of Mother Nature.

There is something so delightfully honest about animals. There is no right or wrong in their world, and they live the life they are meant to. They live with purpose, and spend their days tirelessly striving towards some unspoken goal, without getting bogged down with material possessions or tiresome opinions. They do not carry past hurts or stress over injustices inflicted upon them. There is no malice, no judgment. They are a true example of how to just get on with it. And although the determination to survive is ever present to them, they do not create additional stress by fussing over superficial things.

Yes, birds preen themselves, but I'm quite sure none of them are looking at themselves and saying "I'm fat," "I look terrible," or "I really screwed up by not rising early and getting that worm." They just do what needs to be done. They keep themselves safe, they keep themselves fed, and they do everything they can to ensure the survival of their offspring. There is no histrionic drama, no falseness, no pretense. And when they form a bond with us, we know that their love and affection is pure and unconditional. It comes from their heart and soul.

Family pets provide a great source of satisfaction. Studies have shown that owning a pet can be a wonderful way to relieve stress. If we ever want to experience unconditional love, get a dog. And even pets like fish in an aquarium that do not shower us with affection can calm our thoughts and help us decompress as we watch them glide silently through the water.

We can learn a lot from these beautiful beings with whom we share the planet. Whether we own pets, or just spend time in nature observing wildlife, the quality of our lives is enhanced when we share it with the animal kingdom.

Listen to the story of the White Dutch Clover, with its flocks of tiny bird-like flowers, and enjoy the company of our animal friends.

# Western Wild Bergamot

THE DRY VEGETATION CRUNCHES under my feet as I walk across the hayfield on a late summer's day. A grove of aspen poplars stands sentinel to the north, their trembling leaves creating a light flutter of sound that tickles the soft summer air.

A butterfly appears from out of the violet shadow of the trees, bobbing and weaving its way over the seasoned prairie landscape. Eventually, it finds a spot to rest on the top of a Western Wild Bergamot, but its respite lasts only a few seconds before it takes to the air again.

I remain captivated by the unusual-looking purplish-pink blossoms of the Bergamot. The walnut-sized globes consist of purplish-pink tubes splaying out in all directions. Triangular, pinkish-green leaves grow opposite each other along the length of a dust-colored stem. This flower definitely has a wild look to it.

We all have a secret desire to be extraordinary sometimes, a little on the edge, a bit wild perhaps. But is it the "going wild" part we are seeking, or do we really just want to feel that energy, that passion?

How many of us are living a life of predictability and routine? Our days unfolding like the pendulum of a worn-out clock, swaying slowly back and forth, lulling us into a comfortable fog that makes us inevitably slip into autopilot? Our spirit retreating into hibernation until we become anesthetized? Our lives starting to resemble a pond of still water in which we have stagnated?

How can we live life more passionately? Where do we find the time and energy to be excited about life, and to feel that exhilaration and zest? What is dragging us down and preventing us from letting our spirit soar? There is a heaviness in our heart that is pulling us into a melancholic abyss. Was that heaviness created long ago and sustained by our own embattled thoughts and feelings? What unspoken narrative playing inside our heads is influencing our lives today? Is it gentle and nourishing, or does it continuously attack our soul with its biting, jagged barbs?

Some of us are playing a sad song over and over in our minds, and listening to this broken record as it wails out "I'm not good enough," "My life sucks," or "I hate how I look". Are we even aware of the poison we are steadily feeding ourselves? How can we be passionate and light when we are constantly giving ourselves these messages? No wonder our passionate, vibrant spirit has numbed itself so as not to feel the pain from these sad songs.

There are many of us who received very hurtful and negative messages when we were young and vulnerable. Unfortunately, at that time, we did not realize how those jaundiced actions and words would become firmly engraved on our heart, compelling us to take ownership of them and make them our own personal mantra. Words spoken to us in anger or frustration created very deep and painful tears in our fledgling spirit, and even though we instinctively recoiled from those hurtful phrases, they stuck to us like Velcro. Each word weighed on us and dragged us down.

Eventually, we came to believe those hurtful attacks because they came from people we trusted or admired. If they said those negative things, it must have been because they were true, right? But were they true? Were we lazy? Good for nothing? Would we never amount to anything?

If we did receive those messages, it is important to understand that they came from people who were weighed down with so much bitterness and resentment themselves that they could not possibly appreciate all the good in their world, including us. They lashed out because they had so much hurt in their own heart that it was easier for them to be critical of us rather than fix their own sad, damaged spirits.

Regardless of the source and intention of that spiritual assassination, none of us ever deserved it. Any negative messages we received when we were younger were never true, but we believed them all the same because we were so young and impressionable. Far too many of us are still plagued by those anguished words, but we don't need to believe them now because we are older and wiser.

But what if we are just too worn down to see beyond the hurt? Are we still letting those contaminated messages marinate our spirit in a brine of sorrow? Each time we pay attention to negative messages, we reinforce them, and give them more power and strength with each unconscious allowance.

Fortunately, we can choose to change that. Just as we were compelled to take ownership of those hurtful, negative messages, we can now choose to claim and embrace positive definitions about ourselves. Because our thought patterns were created over a long period of time, they will not change overnight. It will take time and effort, but we are more than up to the task.

Thinking negatively can become a habit, and even though habits are difficult to break, they are not impossible. Our positive thoughts will need to be mined as the rare jewels they are, and then brought to the surface where they can shine. They need to be cradled like a precious newborn, and nurtured and valued by each breath we take. With perseverance, and by thinking positively every chance we get, a new habit of affirmative thoughts and feelings will solidly entrench itself in our gentle spirit.

As with most things in life, the starting point is within our own heart and soul. When negative thoughts and feelings crop up about ourselves, we must recognize them, understand where they came from, and challenge their validity. We have the power to decide if we want to believe the negative messages or not, and we also have the power to release them. We can root them out by telling ourselves the painful narrative was not true, never was, and never will be. Then we replace it with something that is loving and kind and we consciously and consistently reflect on all the good that is within us until our true self is unburdened by all of the past recordings.

As we begin to recognize and appreciate our own beautiful spirit, we can reinforce this process by looking at the bright side of every situation in which we find ourselves. Try to find the humor or the kindness. Try to find the light. There are certainly moments in our lives that are extremely difficult and challenging, and it is okay to feel angry or sad when these times crop up, but it is important to keep things in perspective and, as difficult as it may be at the time, to trust God and try to look for something good. We will find it.

Making positive statements, either out loud or secretly to ourselves, sets a kinder tone and puts us on a gentler course. This new way of thinking may not produce grand results at first, and in fact they may seem negligible, but we must start the evolution because the more we look for good things, the more good things we will find, both in the outside world and, most importantly, within ourselves.

The more we release the negative messages and acknowledge all that is good in our world, the sooner the gloomy cloud that suppresses and weighs down our spirit will weaken. A light, energetic force will begin to flow in our lives and manifest itself in the way we feel and behave. A beautiful light will begin to shine from within and, like an infant dawn, reawaken our spirit to the wonderful possibilities that have always existed within us. We will start to feel brave and strong, and begin to have the courage to release the people and things in our lives that used to bring us down. Our confidence will grow, and we will be ready to live on our own terms, with a spring in our step and a sparkle in our eyes. There will be energy, there will be movement, there will be light, and our passionate, adventurous spirit will finally unfold its lusty wings and soar.

Let us take our lives off autopilot, and rejoice in the thrilling adventure that is our life. And like the Western Wild Bergamot teaches us, let's live our lives with energy and passion.

# Columbine

Sunlight filters softly through a thicket of aspen poplar leaves, settling on the ground in mottled spots of yellow green. Shadows lay on violet cushions, quite content that the heat of the day has not dared to disturb their respite. The entire scene has the quality of a Monet painting—something lovely and precious.

Quietly tucked among this dappled landscape is the Columbine. Slender green stems stretch up from a bower of dark, pointed-lobed leaves. The blossoms are cylindrical, with creamy-white petals reaching out from five blue-violet sepals. This nodding beauty grows in a secluded environment, very quiet and serene, seemingly lost in reticent thought or contemplation. What can you teach us, dear Columbine?

For many years now we have been listening to others tout the benefits of meditation and mindfulness. Many studies have been conducted that show the physical and emotional benefits of giving ourselves some down time, and focusing on what is going on inside our minds and bodies. But how can we improve our overall health by just sitting for five minutes a day and focusing on our breathing? It sounds very simplistic, but it works. Taking time each day to stop the frantic activity of our racing minds has a tremendous impact.

On a physical level, meditation reduces the release of the stress hormone cortisol. Cortisol is one of the chemicals in our body that is responsible for the "fight or flight" response. It helps us respond to stressful events in our lives, and has, for millions of years, been one of the components that enabled our species to survive. Early humans had to deal with many life and death circumstances, and the fight or flight response helped them to survive those trying times.

We do not have the same stressors today that our ancestors did, but we still have the fight or flight response. Our stressors can linger for a long time if our perceived threat is ongoing, such as problems in our jobs, financial difficulties, or being overloaded with information about all the negative things happening in the world. This ongoing stress releases a constant stream of cortisol that, in turn, affects our physical health by increasing our blood pressure, blood sugar, and cholesterol, suppressing our immune system, and affecting our ability to have a restful sleep. It also causes fluctuations in our weight, and fast tracks the aging process.

By helping reduce the release of this hormone, meditation and being mindful can calm our stress reactions, and reduce our fight or flight responses.

Our brains have been hardwired over millions of years to remember the negative events in our lives. This focus was necessary to help our species survive by teaching our ancestors to remember and bypass unpleasant or harmful things. Learning which plants, animals, and places to avoid played a major role in ensuring the continuation and proliferation of our species.

We still carry that primordial mindset of focusing on the negative, which is why many of us remember clearly the dreadful events in our lives, while most of our pleasant memories remain firmly tucked away deep inside our brain. Having negative thoughts and memories are just a part of being human, and it is okay to feel the emotions connected to them, but when we continually focus on the negativity of our past and ruminate about our future, we can get lost, and our spirit can become paralyzed in a tomb of despair.

Some of us deal with the perpetual onslaught of our negative thoughts by trying to ignore our feelings about them, believing that the hurt and fear will eventually go away if we do not give it any attention. But buried feelings do not go away. They keep surfacing and surfacing, and each time we push them down, they simply come back up into the light, gasping for awareness and understanding. By constantly suppressing our emotions, we cause them to build and build until they fracture and burst from their strained chambers, completely sweeping us away in a tsunami of tears and torment. Oftentimes the triggers for these lashing storms are the slightest, most insignificant things, and not even related to the precipitating distressing event. Nevertheless, our spirit knows those painful emotions must be shed, and will take every opportunity to oust them.

By practicing meditation and being mindful of what we are thinking and feeling, we can sort through the bombardment of thoughts and emotions that can sometimes overwhelm us. With daily practice, our mind will begin to recognize the correlation between what we are thinking and how we are feeling. We will become more aware of our emotions, and start to understand where they are coming from. We will recognize and call out the negative thoughts we are focusing on and sustaining. Then when we fully realize these jaundiced mental invasions, we can emphatically change them to ones that are more positive, and set a kinder tone in our heart and soul.

The more we are able to do all that, the more we are able to manage our thoughts and feelings, and prevent them from running wild and out of control. When our mind and body are calm, and when our thoughts are aligned with our emotions, our true spirit can reign unhindered.

Meditating at least once a day is like weight training. We do not need to lift weights all day long to get results, but by being consistent in the exercise, our muscles will grow, our body will change, and we will become stronger.

That is exactly what happens when we meditate. Our brain physically changes and we become stronger and more resilient. Five minutes of daily meditation will calm our emotions and provide us with more clarity of thought, which will last the entire day and beyond. So even though we cannot do much to change our evolutionary makeup, we can manage our fight or flight response, and live a life that is harmonious and serene. We find a peace that comes with being truly connected to our spirit, ultimately leading us back to God's divine love.

Like the Columbine shows us, let us get back in touch with that place within our heart and soul that sings of tranquility and grace.

# Smooth Aster

THE AIR IS SILENT and still on this warm summer's day as I drive towards town. A light suntanned dust cascades out from behind my car, loitering momentarily above the road before drifting slowly off towards the fields.

Traveling along gravel roads is a part of life in the country. How many times have I driven along this same stretch of road, going to and from town on some agricultural errand? It is as familiar and comfortable to me as an old sweater—always there, always the same. Its furrowed tracks and potholes, though at times aggravating, are somehow reassuring in their ever-present state.

Today, however, I see something new. Lovely patches of bright violet clinging to the sides of the ditch have caught my eye. As I bring my car to a stop, the fine road dust quickly envelops me in a cloud of dusky gray. I wait for the air to clear before opening the car door and stepping out to walk to the side of the road. The ditch is delightfully crowded with Smooth Asters.

I feel as if I have stumbled into a large, joyful party, with all these cheerful-looking flowers smiling up at me. I kneel down and run my fingers along the edge of the petals from one of the blossoms. With their dark-yellow centers surrounded by fringes of slender violet petals, the asters all look like they are wearing frilly party dresses. The pointed oval leaves sprouting from slender, branched stems create a delightful backdrop of bright green. This flower is so fun and delightful that one cannot help but be cheered by it.

Being fun-loving and joyful is the story the Smooth Aster sings. But how many of us are doing that? We have filled our lives with so many errands and chores, and things for which we are responsible. How can we even begin to fill our lives with infectious laughter when most of the time we are either too busy or too tired to even crack a smile?

Of course, there was a time when being happy and cheerful was very much a part of who we were. When we were children and could not wait to get up and start the day, life was full of adventure and possibilities. Certainly we had times that we did not look forward to, like going to school, dentist appointments, or being taken to visit an aged relative and having to sit still and behave. And yet, we never allowed those things to pull us down for long. We always seemed to instinctively know there was going to be something good in those experiences. After sitting in a classroom, there was recess where we could play with our friends. After lying in the dentist chair, we were given a new, colorful toothbrush and perhaps some stickers. And visiting an aged relative almost always produced some delicious cookies or a piece of cake.

As children, we had little trouble finding the bright side of things, but unfortunately, as we grew older, many of us lost that ability. And because it can be very challenging to find the bright side of anything when we are constantly shrouded by the heavy robes of responsibility, worry, and stress, that is exactly why it is even more important to look for those bright spots in our lives.

Living a life that is full of joy and love is all about gratitude. Our life is a gift from God, and as with all gifts, it is important to give thanks. If we focus on our blessings and appreciate what we have instead of lamenting what we do not, it will open up our hearts to the tremendous love and wonderment that exists all around us. There is no guarantee this gift will be here tomorrow, which is why it is so important to acknowledge and appreciate what we have been blessed with today, at this very moment.

When we slow down and take the time to look at our life through grateful lenses, we will find blessings beyond measure. Our unique and beautiful body that allows us to move and hold

## Smooth Aster

our precious loved ones is a gift. Our keen and curious mind that allows us to learn and become wise is a gift. Our irrepressible and magnificent spirit that brightens everything it touches is a gift.

When we can see the blessings around us and within us, our heart awakens to more of the wonderful possibilities that are just waiting to be explored. The more things we are thankful for, the more things we will find that will fill our hearts with joy.

Let us begin to take time every day to acknowledge all the blessings in our life—things to smile about, things that make our heart sing. They are all there waiting to be celebrated. Gratitude paves the way for our inner voice to rise and sing. It helps us to get back in touch with the sweet, joyful child we were. To reconnect with that part of our personality that wants to rejoice in all the possibilities of life.

Let us put on that frilly party dress, give thanks for the life we have, and join the Smooth Asters as they gleefully celebrate life.

# Black-Eyed Susan

THE BACK WHEEL ON my old bicycle emits a rhythmic clacking sound as I make my way along the dusty dirt trail that cuts through our field. Savannah Sparrows are trying to outdo the Whitethroats with their melodious tunes. The sound of my bicycle is a rude intrusion into their symphony.

I am on a mission to gather some yarrow for drying. I remember seeing a bunch near the old maple grove, but today something wonderful has distracted me. Black-Eyed Susans have mysteriously appeared near the edge of the small rippling creek that borders our property. I do not remember seeing them last time I was here. I hop off my bicycle and walk through the knee-high prairie grass to get a closer look.

There are at least a dozen florets arching up from one root stock. Purplish-colored stems reach towards the sky, surrounded by pale-green, lance-shaped leaves. The lovely blossoms consist of brownish-black discs, ringed with comely yellow petals. I pluck one of the flowers from its slender stem and gaze into the dark center, its black eye illusively hinting that it harbors a mysterious secret. This enigma is intriguing. What does it know that the rest of us do not?

Having a bit of mystery about ourselves can be very intriguing and alluring. I am not advocating keeping important secrets from loved ones, or being dishonest with people, but not all our thoughts and feelings need to be broadcast to the world. We do not need to share details of our life story with every person we meet. And it is not necessary to expose ourselves to other people's interpretations and judgments of how we have lived our lives and the decisions we have made.

There are issues that are very precious and personal, and opening them up to the masses serves no real purpose other than making us susceptible to people's opinions. What we choose to think and feel is private to us, and we will share if we want, when we want, and with whom we want, and people must respect that space and not pry into areas that are of no concern to them.

Additionally, we do not need to prattle on about every little thing that happens to us. Does the world really need to know what we had for lunch, where we bought our latest pair of shoes, or detail the thought process we endured to decide which color of nail polish to wear? Do we want to be the woman who insists on sharing every detail of her life and laying bare anything and everything she touches, or do we want to exude mystique and enchantment because of our discretion, our gentle, knowing smile, and our deep, stirring eyes? The latter is the woman who is unforgettable, who courageously stands as a beacon, radiating intrigue and excitement.

We want to be seen as composed, intelligent, and self-confident, not grabbing attention from all corners of the world with our constant babbling. Being completely exposed lessens the aura of interest that surrounds us. We want others to believe there is more to us than meets the eye, and more to find out, if they can.

In order to exude that mysterious bouquet about ourselves, we must first be confident and true to who we are. Self-confidence allows us to stand calm and secure, knowing we have a strength of spirit and wisdom to handle whatever life throws at us. When we have self-confidence, there is no reason for us to conform to the masses. We do not need to compete for attention because we know there is nobody else on earth like us. We are unique. We will have no need to plaster our lives all over the place, like dime store posters stapled to signposts advertising things most people do not want. We will have no desire to fill every open space with a verbal barrage of benign facts about our day. There is something extraordinary about us, and keeping those exquisite parts of us protected, sharing only what we choose to share, gives us a very alluring, unforgettable presence.

Having self-confidence allows us to voyage through life feeling more relaxed and level-headed, and it is this perception that gives us an aura of courageousness and serenity, even in the worst of storms. Others will marvel at our composure, wondering what has made us so strong, so resolute. "How does she do it?" they will ask. These characteristics heighten the essence of mystique that surrounds us. There is power in mystery. It makes us very provocative and unforgettable.

Hang onto your secret, dear little Black-Eyed Susan, and thank you for showing us the magic in mystery.

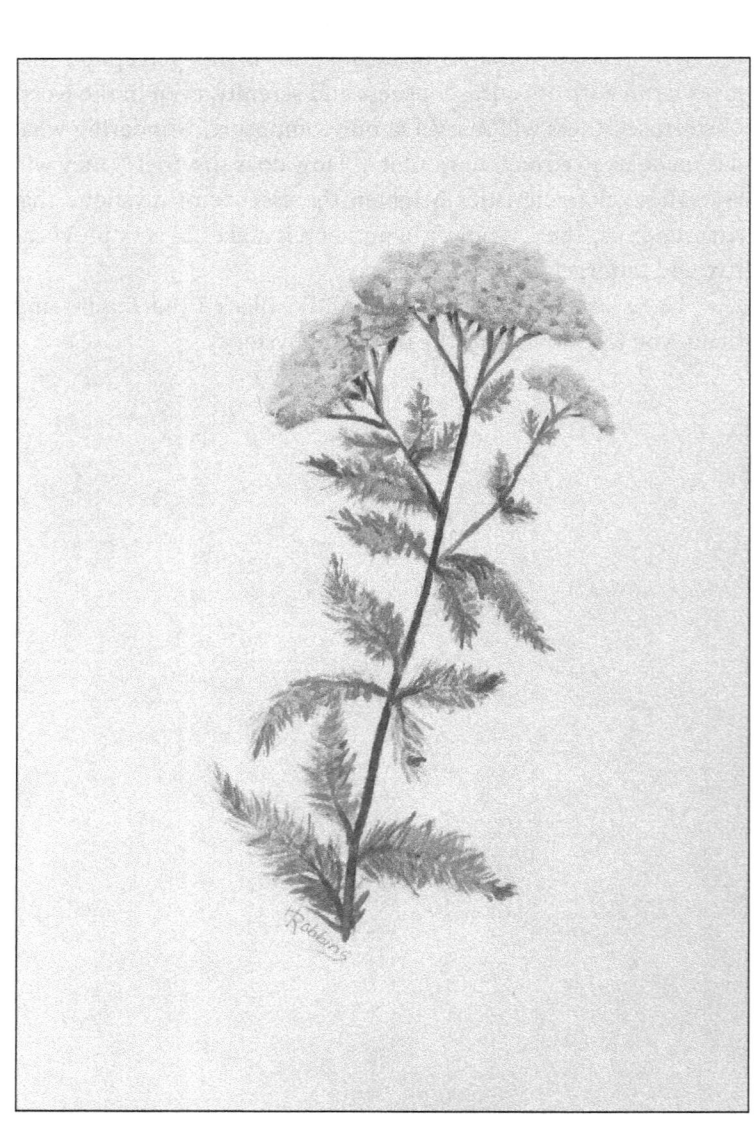

# Yarrow

THE OPEN HILLSIDE SLOPES gently to the south, exhibiting a parade of life that hungrily drinks in the soft rays of the noon-day sun. The trees sway rhythmically in the breeze, as if dancing to an unspoken piece of nature's lyric poetry.

Bobbing their flower heads to this silent beat is a family of Yarrow plants. The blossoms are harmoniously packed together, looking like creamy-white miniature clouds suspended just above the ground. Fern-like leaves tickle the air with their many soft fingers. The tightly knit clusters of the Yarrow blossom speak to me of family. A tight-knit group, springing up from a common root stock.

Family ties bind us together and can help define who we are. Our family can be one of our sources of great joy, swaddling our hearts and providing sanctuary in an unfamiliar and sometimes scary world. Yet as wonderful as our family can be, they can also, at times, be a tremendous challenge. Emotions run very high in families. There is a lot at stake, or so we think. Words of encouragement and love can lift us up so high we can almost touch the clouds. But when the words or deeds from our family hurt us, whether intentional or not, the wound inflicted is very deep and painful, and can last for years.

We have all heard stories about family members who no longer speak to each other due to some transgression, or others who yell and scream or hurl insults and cry whenever they are together. When we peel back the window dressing and look at what is lying underneath any family dispute, we will always find tremendous, overwhelming pain. Pain of having been let down by those we love. Pain of feeling neglected or bullied. Pain of loss. Some deal with this brewing heartache by building monolithic walls of anger and resentment, and shut people out. Others resort to screaming matches whenever they are within earshot of the offending individual.

There are no easy answers when dealing with family conflicts because we are emotionally invested in them. We care what our family members think of us and our actions. We seek out their love and approval, whether we want to admit it or not. And that is why when things go awry, the wounds inflicted sting so much more than those from other offenders we have to grapple with in our lives.

We must remember that our family members are probably doing the best they know how, and like every human being, ourselves included, they will make mistakes and say and do things that will not be acceptable to us. But their words and actions are only as bad as we make them out to be.

Sometimes we have to step back and let people find their own way, and not get caught up in their drama. We may feel the need to put in our two cents, and say or do things to help our family members live a better life. That's a good thing if our input is welcome, but if it's not, then we need to back off. Our family members have their own journeys to attend to, just as we have ours, and if we want them to respect us and our space, we must also respect theirs.

When people say or do things that hurt us, when they throw accusations around like confetti with little or no thought to where each one lands and the damage they can cause, then we need to clearly and specifically let them know what we will and will not tolerate. And instead of hurling insults back at them, calmly explaining to them how their words and/or actions make us feel will redirect the conversation to what is real and what is being damaged. Sometimes people simply need to be made aware of the hurt that is being caused as a result of their careless behavior, so keeping the focus on our feelings will provide greater motivation for change than simply tossing more hurtful words around.

## Yarrow

Whatever happens, or whatever has happened, we need to remember that, like God's love for us, our family's love is present and true. Sometimes it may not be readily apparent, and there might be a lot of screaming and yelling, or years of silence, but there is always love there. Some of us may have to look very hard and with an understanding heart to see it, but it is there.

Love is the root from which the family grows, and regardless of what happens in our lives, we are inevitably drawn back to that root. We may not be pulled back physically, but we will always maintain a connection emotionally and spiritually. Whether we know it or not, we are forever shaped by that love.

Like the Yarrow, let us try to stay close and work at maintaining good feelings with our family. We do not have to always agree, but let us not allow anything to tear us apart. We all need a safe haven in which to harbor our hearts.

# Western Red Lily

The landscape has taken on a dreamy quality today. Like an impressionist painting, the green of the grasses and the orange of the lilies blend fluidly together, painted by soft strokes of creamy glaze, richly displayed on an artist's palate.

My heart is light and my spirit filled to overflowing because I have come across a grove of Western Red Lilies. They are all in bloom and radiant in their finery like ladies at a fancy dress ball. I am afraid to pick one, as it would feel like I was breaking some unwritten code of Victorian etiquette.

Elegance and grace is what strikes me about this flower. The orange petals have a smooth, waxy finish, like the well-pressed satin skirt of a ball gown. Nearer the center, the orange fades to soft yellow, and is peppered with black spots. Stems stand very erect, with many lance-shaped leaves clinging along its length.

Lilies are always so elegant and graceful, without any pretense or fuss. We can learn a lot from the example of the lily in our manner of dress and how we present ourselves to the world. Our style of dress can be a wonderful accompaniment to our unique and beautiful spirit. When we dress well, when our outward presentation is in sync with our inner spirit and personality, it pays the greatest compliment and respect to who we are. When we care about ourselves and honor our unique being through our style of dress, we show the world our true beauty. Our spirit radiates from us like irrepressible sun rays across the clouds.

Taking care of our outward appearance is a reflection of our self-confidence, and how well we care for our inner selves. When we nurture and value our true spirit, we will naturally make the effort to take better care. We will eat better. We will lovingly maintain our physical body with exercise and proper rest. We will find ways to nourish our mind. Our spirit will easily cultivate a strong connection to God. Paying attention to who we really are, and genuinely fostering feelings of love and acceptance for ourselves, will give us a self-confidence that will help carry us in a strong, graceful, and elegant manner, and the clothes we wear will be a lovely accessory to our beautiful being.

Dressing well and having attractive and tasteful clothes is possible for everyone. One does not have to wear designer labels or break the bank to look good. Dressing well and looking good has nothing to do with economic status or body size. It starts with accepting who we are, regardless of the stage of life we are in. Looking good is all about confidence, and the woman who has a solid grounding of who she is, and a genuine love of herself, radiates a beauty far beyond anything the fashion industry can suggest. When we feel good about ourselves, we naturally look good. Our beauty radiates from our cherished spirit inside, not from an assortment of fabric.

We are so fortunate to be women. Whether we see it or not, we have lovely curves, soft skin, shining hair, and beautiful faces. God has blessed us with such an incredible gift, and fostering gratitude and a genuine love for that divine gift is part of our journey. It is such a shame though that some diminish this natural gift by wearing clothes that do not reflect and enhance who they really are, or by wearing too little and over exposing what was meant to be kept sacred and precious. We do not need to be on display. That is not the kind of attention that will lead us to a good place . If we do not cherish our own bodies, how can we expect others to do the same and treat us respectfully? It is up to us to establish what is acceptable and what is not. We want to clothe ourselves in such a way that graciously celebrates our divine body and spirit.

Regardless of our personal style, the clothes we wear enhance the magnificent spirit that exists within each of us. Let us show gratitude and respect for the incredible women we are.

## Western Red Lily

Like the Western Red Lilies, let us stand proud in our lives. Let us celebrate the glorious beauty that God has so divinely gifted within us, and move through our lives wearing clothes that truly express the elegant and graceful women we are.

# Gaillardia

THE DAWN UNFOLDS SLOWLY, creaking open like a well-loved book that leaves us to wonder what stories will be revealed this day. The nimble sunrise skips rays of golden green over fields glistening with dew. Only the trill of a Black Chinned Sparrow rings through the silence, but it is quickly absorbed into the redolent air of early morning.

Peeking out from behind the tall damp grass, the bright face of the Gaillardia greets the day. Its yellow-orange petals radiate a robust, healthy glow that surrounds a crimson velvet globe. This blossom always reminds me of a strong pulsating heart, every beat bursting forth with healing energy. The Gaillardia tells the story of our physical well-being and the importance of maintaining good health.

Many of us take our health for granted, and it is only when we get ill or injured that we give it much attention. We have no problem finding time to fuss over our appearance, or spending hundreds of dollars on creams and lotions to help us look good, but when it comes to what is inside—our blood, organs, muscles, and bones—most of us do not give it much thought. We just assume that things are being taken care of. No news is good news, right?

Lucky for us, our bodies do strive at all times to heal and remain strong and well. They are magnificent machines, but like all machines, they can break down, and we are responsible for putting in the effort to maintain them. Our body has to carry us through what is hopefully a very long life, but it is primarily up to us how we want that life to unfold.

Every day, each of us must decide what we give attention to in our lives, and whatever we decide, there will be consequences. If we fill our bodies with low-nutrient fatty processed foods and sit all day long, our bodies will become sluggish and we will put on weight. Our blood will have difficulty flowing and our organs will become stressed and prone to disease. Our skin will sag and our muscles will atrophy. These are the consequences of an unhealthy lifestyle.

Alternatively, if we fill our bodies with high-nutrient whole foods and exercise regularly, our bodies will be trim and have energy. Our muscles will be firm and our skin will glow from the oxygen that is easily carried through our veins.

I like to think of the body as a vessel that carries our spirit around. And since nobody was put on this earth to take care of us throughout our entire lifetime, that means we are responsible for how well our vessel is maintained. Do we want to head out into the Atlantic Ocean in a ship that is overweight, full of holes, a sputtering engine, and listing to the point that any large wave could capsize and sink it? Or do we want to head out in a strong, sound, even-keeled ship with a robust, energetic engine? Do we want to spend our journey putting out fires and furiously bailing water to stay afloat, or do we want to enjoy the ride? That is a choice only we can make.

How many of us have decided we are too busy to take care of ourselves right now? Exercise takes time. Preparing whole foods takes time. Meditation takes time. Why would we sleep for eight hours when we can get by on six? We are busy people with places to be and things to do. All these points are true, and I am sure most of us have said them to ourselves many times.

The bottom line, however, is how do we want the story of our life to unfold? Do we want to live a long and happy life full of energy and enthusiasm? Do we want to eliminate or at least minimize the amount of pain we feel? Do we want to be active and have mobility at every age? Do we want to set an example for our children and grandchildren so they, too, will live well and age gracefully?

We know what we need to do to be healthy because we are inundated with advertisements and information about maintaining healthy lifestyles. But what will it take before most of us really heed this lesson? How much more time do we think we have to gamble with our health? Are we overwhelmed? Are we unmotivated? Or is there a subconscious mind process telling us we do not deserve good things in our lives?

We all deserve good things in our lives, but we are the ones that need to believe that and start the ball rolling. We do not have to start exercising at the level of an Olympic athlete or scrupulously calculate the nutritional value of everything we put in our mouths. In fact, the best way is to start small, take baby steps, and set attainable goals each day. We just need to move our bodies a little more today than we did yesterday. We need to cut back on the junk and increase the amount of nutritious foods we eat. Just a little each day will make such a difference in how we think and feel. As our body gets stronger, our motivation and enthusiasm will become stronger, and before we know it, eating well and exercising regularly will be a mainstay in our daily lives. The only regret we will have is that we did not start sooner, but at least we will have started.

God has blessed us with a body that is like a precious and magnificent machine, but it is not indestructible. We must take the steps to look after it. When we cherish our body and health, we will be rewarded with energy and vitality.

Like the robust Gaillardia tells us, take charge and let good health radiate in our hearts and glow in our lives.

# Hedge Bindweed

A SLENDER VINE THREADS itself among a bower of chokecherry branches, tenderly wrapping and weaving itself around burnished stalks and dark-green leaves.

Looking very delicate on its own, the Hedge Bindweed unfolds and flourishes within the protective haven of the cherry tree. Its leaves look like the sharpened darts of Cupid's arrow, ready to be plucked and shot towards an unsuspecting love. Funnel-shaped flowers of creamy white cradle a center of pallid-yellow stamens, looking a lot like gauzy paper lanterns glowing in a twilight summer sky. What can we learn from this intriguing wildflower as it curls its tendrils tenderly around the sturdy stock of the cherry tree? What lesson is in store for us?

By the time we become young adults, most of us turn our attention to finding a life partner—someone who will be there to share the rhapsody of our lives, to love and to hold, to laugh with, to lean on when we cry. Being part of a couple can enrich our lives immensely, but for a lot of us, it can also be laced with perplexing challenges. The intertwining of two lives into one requires tremendous patience, diplomacy, respect, and above all, a solid understanding of who we are as individuals.

How many of us have tried to "fit" into our partner's life, doing what we can to accommodate them at the expense of neglecting our own wants and needs? Sometimes it just seems easier to "go along" and not rock the boat. But then that one unfortunate occasion of "going along" turns into two, then ten, then twenty, and before we know it, we are so wrapped up in our partner's domain that we have completely lost sight of our own unique path. We find ourselves swallowed whole, a veritable carbon copy of someone else. This can happen so slowly and over such a long period of time that we may not even realize it until years later.

This is not the journey God intended for us. Instead, it is a road paved with anxiety. The fear of being alone whispers a seductive and sorrowful melody to our sensitive heart, drowning out the sweet music that our own gentle soul is meant to sing. This fear clouds our judgment, and creates an atmosphere of unease, as though we are wandering lost and alone beneath a dark, moonless sky.

To abate that fear of being alone, we search high and low to find a partner, and when we find one, we hold on so tightly to them that we forget to pay attention to ourselves. We make sacrifices in our lives and take on more responsibility for the survival of the relationship than we should. We justify this lifestyle choice by telling ourselves that at least we are not alone. At least someone wants us. We are lovable.

It is true that being part of a couple requires some sacrifice, and that being attentive to our partner's needs and meeting them halfway is a good thing. But what are we sacrificing in order to have that life mate?

When we shut out our own unique spirit, we are headed for trouble. And how many of us have done this, only to discover years later that our neglected spirit has been completely starved of self-nurturing, healthy oxygen? Things cannot survive without oxygen, and so it is when we disregard our heart and soul. There will be some point in our lives when our unique and beautiful being will need to reach out and take in a breath of air.

When we neglect ourselves and our own desires and needs, resentment inevitably starts to encroach upon us. Like wind-whipped embers, it is only a matter of time before the flames of anger and pain lash out, turning everything that was once beautiful in our relationship into a solemn pile of ash. The solution to this is to not let it get to that point in the first place, but if it has, and we have for years acquiesced to our partner, then the time has come to change this behavior.

## Hedge Bindweed

We can start by realizing we have a voice, and that our wants and needs are just as important and valid as those of our partner. We do not need to dig in our heels and refuse to do all the things we did before, but we can start to exert some of our own will. After all, it is our life. This may feel very selfish at first, especially if we have taken the back seat for years and let someone else do the driving. But tending to our own wants and needs is not about selfishness; it is about survival.

God sent our spirit to this place to express itself, learn from others, and share its own unique knowledge. We diminish ourselves when we shy away from our own distinctive journey, and if we deny the world our spirit, our insights, and our wisdom, then everyone is denied our gifts, especially us. We can begin forging our own true pathway by listening to our heart, and discovering the things we would like to do or the places we would like to go.

This may come as a surprise to our partners at first, but if they truly accept and respect us, they will probably be glad that we are sharing our magnificent spirit with the world—the same beautiful spirit they were drawn to in the first place. If our partners balk at the very idea of supporting our new course, then we must be prepared to do these things on our own or with a friend. It does not have to mean the relationship is over, but each of us is responsible for living our lives on our own terms, which means we have every right to seek out those things that will bring us joy and fulfillment.

Making a relationship work requires both parties to take ownership for its survival, but we are only responsible for the part we have to play. It is important to love and respect our life partner, accept who they are as an individual, and try to understand the path they are traveling on their journey. But we must love and respect ourselves first and foremost, and understand our own path in life. How can we possibly express loving feelings for our partners if we have not fostered those feelings for ourselves? And how do we open up and give the best that is within us if we do not believe there is anything of value in us to give in the first place?

We need to discover and support all the beautiful and unique qualities within us, just as God does. We need to believe absolutely that we are worthy of love and are lovable. When we do that, when we wholly and completely understand it, the beautiful attributes that have always existed within us will grow stronger, and we will no longer fear emptiness or being alone. Self-love and respect for ourselves fills our spirit to the point of overflowing. When our heart is full of love and acceptance of ourselves, it naturally spills over and touches everyone around us. Our relationships will be enriched because we are letting our beautiful spirit soar.

There are no guarantees in the game of love. No iron-clad guarantee that our relationship will go the distance. The only assurances we have in life is that when we pay attention and honor our own true and beautiful spirit, we will never lose ourselves in the tangle of life's garden. Our life is our own. We can only travel along the path we forge for ourselves, and only we have the power to decide where that path will go. Naturally, we hope it will run nicely alongside our partner's path, but it will still be ours. And, as with all paths, there will be bumps and snags along the way, but when we walk with courageous and confident footsteps towards our own destiny, are true to ourselves, and honor our spirit, we will never get lost.

The story of the **Hedge Bindweed** teaches us an important lesson in relationships. As it grows, it embraces the loving support of the cherry tree, intertwining its slender tendrils throughout, but not clinging so tightly that it chokes the life out of the tree. It relies on the tree for support, but not its life. It does not completely lose itself in the bower of cherry leaves. The white blossoms shine unhindered as it maintains its own unique spirit.

Similarly, our goal should always be to stand in the light with our partner, not exist in their shadow. To compliment each other, not be a carbon copy. To be there for each other, loving and supportive.

Let us listen to the story of the Hedge Bindweed and journey down the path that is there just for us without sacrificing the wonderful qualities that make each of us a unique and beautiful being.

# Plains Prickly Pear Cactus

IN ORDER TO SURVIVE in the dry prairie landscape, plants must be strong and resilient, just like the Plains Prickly Pear Cactus. With its large teardrop-shaped stems covered with sharp spines, the Cactus grows in clustered colonies on prairie hillsides. In June and July, light lemon-yellow blossoms burst from the top, showing uncharacteristic softness against the harshness of the needles. This plant is as beautiful as it is strong and resilient. Nobody messes with a cactus.

Like the Plains Prickly Pear Cactus, women have had to grow on difficult and at times inhospitable landscapes. But not only did we grow, we thrived. God gave women the ability to adapt and make the best of any situation, which has become one of our trademarks. Our ancestor mothers honed these qualities which have been blessedly passed down through the generations. These courageous and wise women could not rely on physical brute strength to survive, and instead had to depend on their intuition and wisdom. Women did not have the solid body mass and strength to resolve conflicts by physical means, and so learned to think through any problems. Early women had to remember which foods were fit to eat and where the waterholes were, and to look after the children and keep the family clothed, all while watching out for ever-present dangers. They were teachers, healers, peacemakers, and confidants. As a result, our wonderful ancestor mothers developed keen minds, capable of tackling many tasks at once. It is these phenomenal attributes that we have inherited and possess today.

How many of us are raising children, keeping house, fulfilling social commitments, and working at jobs that bring in the family income? Women have proven time and again that we can jump into any arena and do what is necessary to succeed. We now run corporations, fly in space, cure diseases, hold public office, participate in contact sports, and the list goes on and on. We are more than capable of holding our own in the world. But let us not forget that even though we can participate equally to men, we do not want to be men. Men are great human beings with their own wonderful qualities, but we need to hold on to and cherish those unique qualities that we, as women, possess—our gentleness, kindness, and compassion. We can be strong and independent, yet still be soft and nurturing. And we need to be both respected for our intelligence and admired for our gentleness.

Women have had to jump over many hurdles to get to where they are today, and there are still more hurdles to face. One impediment we must overcome is that sometimes we do not treat each other as well as we could. Women can be the greatest friends and allies, but we also have a tendency to tear each other down. We can sometimes be spiteful and cruel and even catty to each other, and I've often wondered if this tendency has been carried with us since early times in our human experience.

When we look at nature programs featuring troops of primates or prides of lions, there is a definite hierarchy among the females. The higher the female in the hierarchy, the better the chance she and her offspring have of survival. Is it possible that the "pecking order" mentality is a primordial characteristic that women have been unconsciously passing down through the generations? Do we still harbor a version of this today, and does it manifest itself when we put each other down?

Regardless of the foundation and the reasons for its existence, it really is tiresome. And it serves absolutely no purpose in this day and age, nor does it help to advance us on our incredible journey. We know better and we can do better.

Life on this earth can be very challenging for women. We have enough knocks to deflect in this world without additional strife from our sisters. Why make things more difficult? We should try to always support each other. We must nourish our collective spirit so we can continue to strive en masse towards a peaceful and glorious future for all of us. When we see a woman who has succeeded at something, let us be genuinely happy for her instead of picking at her personality or appearance. We have no idea what that successful woman has been through, what demons she has had to face, or which negative internal messages about herself she grapples with. Tearing her down does not simultaneously lift us up to loftier heights. If anything, it pushes us further down into the muck. We need to continually lift each other up, and pave the way for our daughters and granddaughters to follow.

Remember that there are many little girls with big, curious eyes watching us at this very moment, eagerly absorbing and learning from the example we provide. We need to show them that all women are valuable and worthy of respect and support.

When we have the self-confidence to accept and respect our life journey and that of our sisters, we will help to create heaven on earth. Women have such an important part to play in the success of our species, as we lead the way with God's guidance and our strength, compassion, wisdom, and love.

Like the Plains Prickly Pear Cactus, let us continue to be strong, independent and resilient, while maintaining a softness and beauty that is unique to us all.

# Prairie Coneflower

It is one of those hazy summer days where the horizon dances and melts in the heat of the noonday sun. Grasshoppers sing their sibilant tunes to each other, creating a high-pitched buzzing that trembles the gossamer spider threads hanging between the branches of the willows.

The railroad tracks upon which I find myself have long been abandoned. Their days of transporting people and goods to far-off destinations have slipped silently away, leaving behind fading thoughts of places seen and memories made. I am amazed by the variety of grasses and wildflowers nestled between the rusted steel tracks. They stretch up from the gravel between the rotting ties, and hungrily drink in the rays of the hot summer sun.

Among this rich vegetation is the Prairie Coneflower, and I am compelled to stop and smile at this whimsical little plant. The conical center of each blossom resembles a reddish-brown sewing thimble, surrounded by bright yellow to yellowish-brown petals. This flower can reach two feet in height on pale, leafless stems. A wreath of deeply cleft, light-green leaves rest on the ground, as if cradling this unique and interesting plant.

The Prairie Coneflower is also commonly called Mexican Hat because of its resemblance to the traditional wide-brimmed hats worn in Mexico. In fact, whenever I see it, I am reminded of the many different places and cultures that exist in the world. And because humankind is so rich with interesting and diverse populations, I believe it is important to understand and appreciate that diversity.

# The Wisdom of Wildflowers

Just as a prairie meadow is home to many varieties of plants and animals, so it is with the world and humankind. Imagine what our world would look like if we were all the same color, spoke the same language, practiced the same cultural traditions, dressed the same, drove the same cars, worked at the same jobs, and lived in identical houses to each other. What an incredibly dull world it would be.

Fortunately, as with all living things, our species has evolved to provide a kaleidoscope of colors and characteristics, all molded and shaped by each group's environment and history. Each culture and race is unique with its own distinct qualities and characteristics, just as each individual is unique with their own distinct qualities and characteristics. We are all different, we are all beautiful, and we all deserve to live our best life.

Our forefathers did not always accept and appreciate the wonderful diversity of the human race, and I cannot even imagine the number of conflicts throughout history that have resulted from their intolerance.

We now know that prejudices stem from fear. Some of our ancestors did not understand the uniqueness of other cultures, and they let their fear of the unknown cause them to behave atrociously. Unfortunately, there are still some individuals and communities that continue to harbor outdated supremacist views. And it seems such a shame that in this day and age where we have advanced to cure diseases and explore outer space, there are those who are so fearful and cling to discriminating and biased ideals. There are still far too many out there who continue to criticize another culture's customs or judge someone based on the color of their skin. Is it not time to move beyond this antiquated, territorial, narrow-minded way of thinking and behaving?

If we find ourselves surrounded by these toxic, exclusionary thought patterns, let us be the ones to say "That's enough." Let us join with those who have gone before and continue to bring positive change and inclusion within our own families and communities. We are all God's children and we all have a place here.

Just as it is important to understand who we are and strive to accept ourselves unconditionally, we also need to understand others and accept who they are. Remaining silent and going along with the status quo is no longer acceptable. We need to educate ourselves about the other cultures and races with whom we share this planet, and when we do that, we will understand why people look like they do, speak the way they do, and believe the things they do. With that understanding, appreciation and respect will naturally follow.

By being aware of other cultures, we become more tolerant and understanding towards our fellow human beings. That is the way God intended for us to live in peace with one another. When we understand and accept all races and cultures, a depth and richness will flow in our lives that comes from having an intelligent, open mind, free from fear of the unknown. And when we know and appreciate how others live, we will come to know and appreciate the blessings in our own lives.

Like the Prairie Coneflower tells us, let us open our hearts and minds, and embrace the richness of our world.

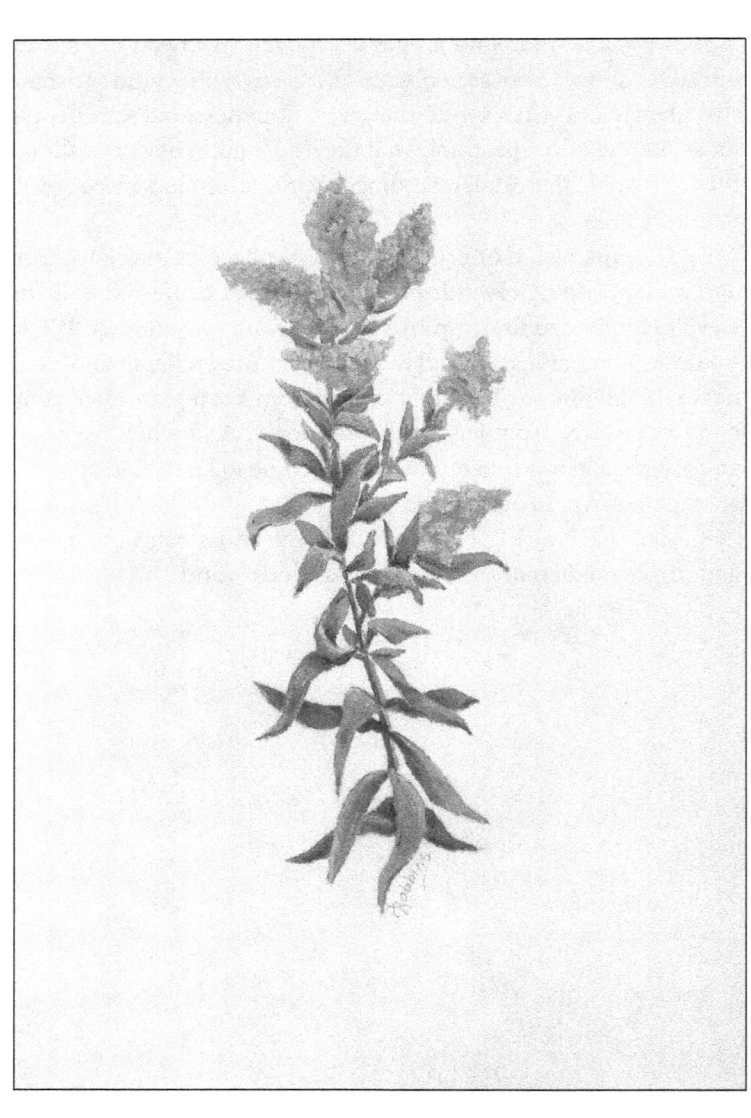

# Velvety Goldenrod

THE MEADOWS ARE TINGED honey brown as summer reaches its ripening season. Grasses have lost their glorious green glaze, now looking duller and slightly worn, like an old sweater whose crispness has been transformed into something comfortable and reassuring.

Swaying rhythmically in the gentle breeze, the Velvety Goldenrod stands tall among the meadow vegetation. Rich, yellow blossoms arranged in the shape of a pyramid are perched on top of thick woody stems. Pale-green, lance-shaped leaves cling to the sides, dressing the entire length of the plant.

Do we stand tall in our lives like the Goldenrod in the meadow? Do we have dignity and honor? Do we respect others as well as ourselves? Are we living a life that allows us to be honest and true, or are we living a life that is false? How many of us are hiding behind a mask, pretending to be someone we are not, and participating in things just to gain the approval of others?

If we truly valued and respected ourselves, we would not be playing these games. When we steadfastly honor and value who we are, we will always do the right thing by ourselves. We will make the right decisions because we have put our thoughts and feelings at the forefront. By valuing and respecting what we think, feel, and do, we will stand tall, strong, and proud in life's meadow.

People who do stand tall, strong, and proud are not thought of as being liars, gossipers, or cheaters. We see them as having integrity, class, and grace. When we have dignity and honor, we walk a higher road. We walk closer to God and are lifted out of the petty muck that too many people seem happy to wallow in.

Having dignity and honor also helps us to see things more clearly because we will not let deception cloud our judgment and drag us down. We will not tell lies because that taints our own spirit. Telling a lie is like taking a beautiful marble statue and smearing mud all over it. The statue is still there, but now it is dirty and ugly. When we lie, we smear ourselves with that same muck. It makes us ugly, and is not who God wants us to be.

And why would we need to lie anyway? What is it about our beautiful being or the decisions we make that we feel we need to be false about? If we are being true to ourselves, respectful, and kind, we won't need to distort who we are or what we are doing. If we are feeling vulnerable and scared or not feeling good enough, seeking God's guidance and treating ourselves as he would—gently and with love—is the only thing that will help fill the void in our soul. Trying to fill the emptiness with lies and falseness is like trying to fill up a sieve with sand. The facade will never stick for long, and we will have to continue with the deceit to fool ourselves, and the world, into thinking we are whole. We will never be beautiful and whole when we tell lies.

As with lying, spreading malicious gossip tarnishes our dignity. When we participate in gossip, we are telling the world that our own life is shallow and unfulfilled. When we talk others down, we are essentially saying that we are better than them and therefore entitled to our haughty judgments. But when we indulge in this petty activity, we are not better than the person we are talking about. In fact, we are actually worse because we should know better.

When we gossip, we are simply demonstrating that we lack the gracious kindness and compassion that God has instilled in our soul. Our spirit has a huge hole in it that we are trying to cover up with ridiculous stories about others. If we keep the focus on someone else, or on their problems or perceived imperfections, then the world will not see the vulnerable, scared women that we are, and we can continue deluding ourselves, and those around us, that all is well in our lives. When we focus on what we perceive are the gossip-worthy problems of others, we are not focusing on our own problems that need attention. We are not looking within at our good qualities that require nurturance and support. We are not facing our own demons. Sometimes it is easier to look outside of ourselves, point fingers, and whisper than it is to fix what is broken within us.

When we stand tall with dignity and honor, we also won't become romantically involved with someone who has made a commitment to another. When we have affairs, it says that we are insecure, hollow, and will seek out attention from anywhere. Mistresses are always in second place. They are "on the side." What is the value of something that is kept on the side? Do we not deserve to be in first place? Do we not deserve to stand strong and proud alongside the partner of our choice, rather than slink around and exist underneath the dark cloak of deceit? Our beautiful being did not come to this world to be somebody's "seconds."

It is important to choose partners who will value and respect us every day. Should we really trust someone who is cheating on their significant other? Are they not showing us that they are more than capable of deception? When we meet these people who are committed to someone else, we need to be clear that we are not interested in being the solution to filling their hollow souls, or padding their fragile egos. We deserve so much more, and when we truly believe that, when we honestly know how valuable we are, we will avoid these fraudulent scenarios. Leave those misguided souls to get their own houses in order before they come knocking on our door.

God wants all of us to have love, to have a rich and rewarding life, and to always be number one, and we can have all these things when we decide we are worthy of it. When we decide not to gossip. When we decide not to cheat. When we decide not to lie. When we decide to love the honorable woman we are, and were always meant to be, we can work on creating a life around that.

When we value ourselves, we will not need to be false, to gossip, or be anyone's second best. The hole in our soul that we tried to fill with love and approval from others will simply not exist. Our love for ourselves will fill us up to the point of overflowing. We will have confidence and stand so tall that we will be beacons for others to follow. We will be proud to show our daughters, granddaughters, and all young girls how to live a beautiful life that is honorable and true. Let us show the world our dignity and honor. Let us show the world our grace.

As the story of the Velvety Goldenrod tells us, we can all stand tall in our glorious meadows.

## Scarlet Paintbrush

THE AIR IS PERFUMED with a myriad of flora and fauna. Honey bees skip from wildflower to wildflower, gathering what they require to make their liquid gold. The sounds of their buzzing gently caresses the surrounding countryside, lulling all who live there into a gentle, bucolic dream.

My horse is oblivious to the bee's labors as she walks lazily through the long grass, occasionally grabbing a mouthful of the succulent green blades.

We make our way into a shaded glen on the pretense of looking for stray cattle, but instead, my attention is drawn to a cluster of Scarlet Paintbrushes. What a delight to come upon these unique blossoms. I rein my horse, who is more than happy to stop and lunch on the vegetation, and I slide out of the worn, creaking saddle.

The Scarlet Paintbrush is distinctive with its wavy red petals clinging along the top of long, burgundy stems. Aptly named, they resemble well-used paint brushes with bristles splayed out in all directions. It is always a special treat to come across this wildflower, partly because it is not as common as some of the other blossoms in this region, but also because it speaks to the more creative side of life.

Humans have been creating since the dawn of their existence. It is one of the main characteristics that has set our species apart from the other living beings with which we share this planet. Expressions of creativity touch all of us because it exists within all of us. There is a creative wellspring that inhabits the conscience of every living soul, and expressing that creativity is necessary for our emotional, and ultimately physical, health and well-being.

Engaging in creative activities allows us to tap into our innermost world and bring it into the light. By exploring this beautiful world within us, we find wonderful treasures that we perhaps did not know existed. The more we drink from this creative wellspring, the stronger it will flow, sweeping us into an incredible world of imagination, illumination, and inspiration.

If they are not readily apparent, it is extremely important to take the time to discover our own unique creative attributes, and to identify the talents flowing in our creative wellspring as it languidly entwines its way through our soul. Unfortunately, many talents are never uncovered and shared because people have crushed their creative springs before they were given a chance to flow. They look at well-known artists and declare, "I can't paint like him" or "I can't sing as well as her" or "I can't compose like so and so," and they never try to explore their own inherent creativity.

We all need to remember that creativity is not a competition. We do not have to produce an item for the world to praise and then pay us big bucks for. In fact, being creative is not about the end result at all; it is the process that is important. Think of the legendary pot of gold at the end of the rainbow. The gold is nice, no question, but the rainbow is where the beauty lies. The rainbow is what inspires and lifts us up. Also, we do not need to paint or sing or dance like a professional. If our soul is nudging us to paint, then we pick up a brush and we paint, and simply by engaging in that activity, we pay homage to our spirit and our Creator, and become more aligned with our authentic self.

Whichever activity or creative endeavor we pursue, it is the movement and the force that is important. They enable us to explore the depths of our creative spirit and courageously dive in and pull from within all that is exquisite and unique about ourselves. We are all one of a kind in this world, and whatever we create will be divinely distinctive. We create what is in us to create.

By dedicating time to the creative process, our emotional and physical well-being will flourish with the nourishing presence of a fulfilled and whole spirit. This process helps us to discover more about ourselves—what we like, what we love, what brings us joy. This inward focus helps to strengthen and nurture all that is good and right within us. And when we are ready, when we are confident about our creativity, we will want to bring it to the world. We will want to share with others the beautiful gifts from our spirit. And like all the creative souls who live now, and all those who have gone before, we will join in a blessed collaboration of beings that bring beauty to our planet. We will be part of a kinship that promotes joy, passion, and inspiration.

But first we must believe. We must believe in ourselves and that our creative wellspring does exist. When we know in the deepest recesses of our being that we have a creative spirit that is full and alive, then we will truly be on the path to wholeness. We will know that we are perfect and complete, and that we always have been and always will be.

Creativity in all its forms helps us to express ourselves in a universal way. It bridges the gap between cultures, languages, and generations. The sharing of souls through art brings harmony to our delightfully diverse planet.

Like the Scarlet Paintbrush tells us, let us find our talent, for it will illuminate the pathway to our unique and beautiful spirit, and allow us share our wonderful gift with the world.

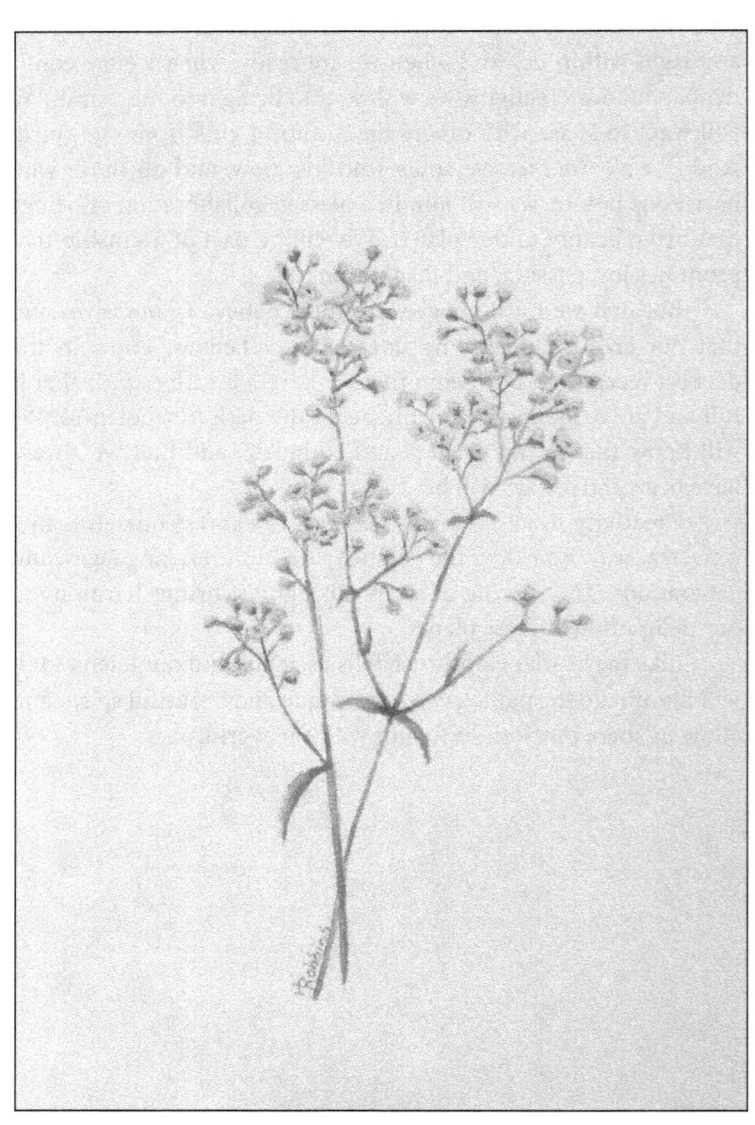

# Baby's Breath

THE CEMETERY. A SACRED place that draws an instinctual reverence. Gravestones lined up in rows, standing silently to attention, mark their passing years with small cracks and mottling hues of aqua and emerald green from the moss and lichen.

One headstone in particular catches my eye. A solemn granite block standing strong and absolute, marking the final resting place of a man I never knew. Carved into the granite face, his name has worn smooth, indicating that his passing occurred some time ago. The dates are barely visible, obscured by a soft mist of Baby's Breath that rises up from the base of the stone. This light and elegant plant likely grew from a wayward seed that fell from a flower arrangement someone had placed in the graveyard years ago.

The soft airiness of Baby's Breath is an exquisite contradiction to the thick, voluminous stone. It is as if the granite is a symbol of the man's earthly body and life, solidly anchored to the land, and the Baby's Breath is his spirit, light and free. This beautiful plant consists of a globe of multi-branched stems sprinkled with hundreds of tiny white flowers. The blossoms consist of five minuscule petals encircling a yellow dot, and are barely noticeable by themselves. But when grouped together, the entire plant has the ethereal look of a soft, wispy cloud where angels would reside.

Although Baby's Breath is not an indigenous flower on the prairies, it can usually be found growing wild along ditches and fields that border rural cemeteries. They serve as delicate harbingers to these sacred places that are the final resting grounds for our loved ones. Seeds spilled from flower arrangements are carried on the prairie winds and scattered on the surrounding countryside, and when the plants are full grown, large, airy globes of soft white flood the landscape.

This plant speaks to me of the more spiritual side of life. We are all on a spiritual journey. But what is spirit really? We can't see it, we can't touch it, we can't smell it, and yet we know it exists. Our spirit is the essence of our being, an intrepid force that radiates from us and sustains us, flowing like a pristine silvery river, wrapping and weaving its way throughout our lives as it navigates its way home to God. It is the one thing we all possess that embodies the truth of who we really are, and it is shared equally by all living things.

The soul is the light that shines in our eyes and radiates from our smiles. It speaks without words, and influences without actions. It is that inner voice that tenderly whispers gentle notes of direction to our conscience, helping to guide us through the journey we know as life.

Our spirit sings to us through our feelings of anxiety, joy, and sorrow, all of which are subtle nudges and cues sent from God. By paying attention and listening to the gentle messages delivered from our sacred Creator, it enables us to make decisions that help us to be courageous and strong. This loving guidance comes to us as intuition, or that "gut feeling." The more we pay attention to these messages, the more honed our connection to our spirit and our God will be, causing us to live more fully and aware. We come into our own because we are whole beings, not purely organic masses of molecules wandering about. We are a living force radiating an essence that rivals the dynamic energy of nature herself.

There are those who do not give spirit much thought. They rush through life acting and reacting to the physicality of their days, shutting out both the gentle directions from God and the subtle clues that are there to guide us. However, recognizing that beautiful spirit and hearing its subtle messages is not always so easy, especially for those who have never been encouraged to see and value it.

## Baby's Breath

There is no "one size fits all" method of making a connection to our spirit. And while there is certainly no shortage of guides willing and able to help, making that strong connection is something each individual has to discover on their own. We all have a unique journey to travel on this earth, and developing and maintaining a strong connection to our spirit and to God is part of that pilgrimage. However we choose to accomplish that purpose is unique to each of us, and because only we get to decide what that is, we know it will be the right choice.

Many of us have to struggle through very dark waters before we recognize God and his love for our eternal, spiritual being. When we finally do, we will understand that our Creator and spirit have always been a part of us. Our spirit is that ever-present essence that has enlightened our lives from the very beginning, and will continue until the physical body has drawn its last breath.

Our spirit is always free, even if our physical bodies are not. When we get tangled and choked with life's stresses, we can draw comfort knowing our God's love for us is steadfast and absolute. Our spirit remains strong and free, and will never abandon our beautiful being. No one else on the planet will ever possess our spirit. It belongs to us alone.

Let us honor our spirit that has helped us to survive somber shadows and to celebrate luminous seasons, and been blessedly present for everything in between.

Like the mist of Baby's Breath in front of the granite gravestone, our spirit radiates from our bodies, and envelops our world in an embrace of beauty.

# Canada Thistle

THE PRAIRIE WIND BLOWS strong from the west today, bending the tall grass with its blustery strokes. The trees appear to dance as their branches twist and sway to nature's eclectic symphony. Walking down the pasture trail is difficult, with dust blowing into my eyes and strands of my hair lashing at my face. A powerful gust of wind hits me and for a moment knocks me off my course. I fight to regain balance before heading on.

Along the rusted barbed-wire fence that parallels the trail lives a tangle of Canada Thistles, doing their best to brave the strong wind. I am amazed at their strength and resolve to remain upright, despite such a difficult, blustery day. The Canada Thistle looks powerful with its strong stem that bears many scalloped-edged leaves with small thorns projecting from each point. Pale-mauve multi-petal blossoms cling tenaciously to the top, holding firm and composed to the sturdy stems.

Even in the worst of storms, the Thistle stands entrenched and confident, maintaining just enough flexibility to help it survive, and even thrive, in a sometimes hostile environment. It reminds me of the tough times in our lives, and all the many prickles and stings we encounter. Those times when we are knocked off our course by strong and sometimes unexpected winds. How can we stay strong and powerful like the Thistle, but not so rigid that we cannot bend to the changing winds in our lives?

Change is the one thing we can all count on. Many of us fear it, and sometimes rightly so. Wary of the unfamiliar, we take comfort in that which is known because we have already lived and survived it. We know what to expect, and we know we can handle it because we have done so before. But when things change, and they will, we are faced with a new set of circumstances. The rules have changed, and it is only natural to feel anxious and wonder how we will handle the new course we find ourselves on.

Because change can be very frightening, we put a lot of energy into resisting it, but that resistance robs us of our true power. Intrinsic strength comes from the knowledge that wherever life takes us, we will be able to face it head on, and deal with whatever comes our way. With God's guidance we can tap into the incredible power ingrained within us, a strength that has been with us from the very beginning. We have relied on that strength on many occasions in the past, and navigated our way through difficult circumstances each and every time they arose. We may have been a little battered and bruised at the end, but we also came out a little wiser and more resilient.

We can still be wary and unsure of what the future may bring, but if we remain flexible and open to each new experience, the energy saved by not resisting the change will be more than sufficient to help us deal with our new course.

Resistance creates constriction in our thinking. Our bodies fall into fight or flight mode, and we react automatically, spontaneously, and not always wisely. Instead of falling into that trap, try to see the changing circumstances from every angle and put it in perspective. What are our options? Where can we look for more information? What is out there for resources and supports? It is important to keep an open mind.

We grow each time we embrace change, and the more we grow, the stronger and more resilient we become. The more we are tested, the more opportunities we have to conquer our fears. Each time we do this, our confidence grows in our abilities and our intelligence. I am sure we can all think of at least one time in our lives where we faced a challenging issue. How did we fare? Are we wiser? Are we stronger? My guess is yes, we did become wiser and stronger, and gained more confidence in our abilities as a result. It is that confidence that strengthens our spirit, and that strength will never abandon us.

There will be times that are difficult and full of prickles and stings, but we will survive. We have made it this far, and with God's love and guidance we will continue. I have seen Thistles that were knocked completely to the ground, yet the blossoms still managed to stretch up towards the sky, refusing to give up on their glorious chance at life.

Like the Canada Thistle, let us face the unknown head on and reach towards our future, regardless of the twists and turns we are likely to encounter along the way. And let us give thanks to God for the strength and resolve that we already possess.

# Penny Cress

I STAND ON THE dusty pasture trail on this hazy September day, and let the sound from the singing birds soak deeply into my soul. Their sweet notes blend fluidly together, creating a breezy melody in nature's ongoing harmonic orchestra. But today, among the beautiful notes from the avian world, there is a light fluttering sound as hundreds of tiny rattles tremble on the delicate autumnal zephyr.

The sound drifts up from the ground near where I am standing. A cluster of Penny Cress have added to nature's symphony with their soft, fluttering seedpods. An interesting looking plant, the Penny Cress has many short stems on which cling dozens of coin-shaped seedpods, all glowing a brilliant copper on this late summer day. The tiny white blossoms that crown the top of the plant are gone now, along with the elongated oval leaves that once attached to the stem. The plant that remains looks like a miniature version of a money tree.

Ah yes, the proverbial "money growing on trees" phenomenon that our parents kept telling us did not exist. Unfortunately, they were right, which is why it is important for us to be responsible when it comes to the money we work so hard to make.

For many generations there were not a lot of opportunities for women to go out and make their own money. Most had to rely on their husbands or birth families to help support them. That did not mean women were not contributing in other crucially important ways, but not being in control of the finances put some women at a disadvantage, and kept them from living the life they desired for themselves. Thankfully, things are changing in this regard, and women have become more financially savvy and independent. With this change, however, also comes additional responsibilities.

In a lot of households, the managing of the finances rests with the women. Fortunately, most of us have inherited an innate ability to manage money, but there are times when we struggle with the undertaking. The basic rule of thumb is to not spend more than we make. This is so simple a concept that it seems silly to even mention it, but sometimes we do not follow this elemental rule.

We live in a society of spend, spend, spend—get what we want now and pay later, put it on the credit card and don't worry about it. It is very easy to be seduced by colorful and exciting ads showing us the spectacular, fun life we can all have if we purchase a certain item. And many of us buy into the fantasy that things will be better as soon as we get that new car, eat at that posh restaurant, or use that expensive hair product.

There is nothing wrong with purchasing things with the money we have worked so hard to earn, but we need to be intelligent about it. It is important to live in the present, look for the positives and strive to be happy, but our finances are an area that needs to be handled seriously. When we are intelligent about our money, it is much easier to live in the present and be positive and happy, but when we are careless with our finances, living well becomes a little more difficult. There is nothing positive or fun about drowning in debt.

Spending money has become far too convenient in this day and age. If each time we wanted something we had to go to the bank and withdraw funds to pay for it, many of us would simply not bother. But these days, we can pull out our debit or credit cards or pay online without blinking an eye. By doing all our financial transactions electronically, we easily lose sight of how much money we actually have in our bank accounts. These days, we do not "see" a collection of coins or notes sitting in front of us, so we cannot watch as lump sums disappear or are taken away.

The electronic age is here to stay, and in fact there are probably not many of us who pay with cash anymore. This is why we need to be mature and diligent about what money we have available when we do consider purchases. We must keep an ever-watchful eye on our account balances, as well as an awareness of what bills will be showing up in the immediate future.

What is more important, buying the cute pair of shoes or paying the rent? Realistically, the shoes can wait, but the rent cannot. And if the shoes are that important, then we can save for them. More often than not, however, after a few weeks, the shoes don't seem as vital to our existence as they were when we first saw them, but at least we still have a roof over our head.

Certainly we should make time to enjoy ourselves, but we also need to make sure we are sheltered and have food to eat. It isn't so easy to look vibrant, happy, and carefree like the people in the ads when we are about to be evicted, or have not eaten a decent meal in three days. Making sure we have a comfortable home and good food to eat is a basic and integral part of taking care of ourselves and our family. When we have the basics looked after, and we have security and comfort, then we can turn our attention to the other parts of our lives that add fulfillment. When we are not secure, our happiness and well-being precariously hang in the balance, ready to be ripped from us at a moment's notice.

If all this sounds severe and serious, that's because it is. We need to make sure our basic needs are met.

If we want to be equal players and respected as such in this world, one of the issues we need to address is taking our finances seriously. We cannot live on the assumption that someone else will take care of us later on. And who wants to be the woman that needs to be taken care of anyway?

Regardless of our living situations, whether we are single or in a committed relationship, we have a very important role to play in the managing of the household finances. We can choose to either steer the ship, or we can go around and poke holes in the hull, leading to a very difficult voyage and an inevitable sinking of the boat.

For those of us who are working for an income, we must keep in mind that the day will come when we will either not want to or not be able to work. What will we do for money then? When we are just starting out in our working careers, it is difficult to imagine what life is going to be like in our later years. We want to live life to the fullest right now and enjoy the money we work so hard to make. Who wants to worry about retirement when in their 20s or 30s?

However, by fully understanding what our financial situation is at the moment, and knowing where we would like to be in five, ten, or twenty years or more, we can develop a plan to enjoy our money now, and yet still manage to put some aside for our future. Opening a savings account and faithfully depositing, say, 10 percent of our income each month will build a nice little nest egg for us.

Indeed, there are many options available for saving and investing that will help our money grow. The part we are most responsible for is to just do it, get it started, and stick with it. This is a very large part of looking after ourselves today and in the future.

In my mind, the term "savings account" is more of a "security account." Just knowing we have a pot of money tucked away can give us tremendous comfort. When we have some savings set aside we will be more prepared for whatever comes along. Having that nest egg can give us options, and the more options available, the more control we will have. We may not be able to entirely direct how events unfold in our future, but whatever happens, we will be okay because we have made a plan and will be in the driver's seat. Remember, having savings is the one thing we can do that is entirely for ourselves. It will be there for our security, peace of mind, and in some cases, even safety. But again, that security account will require us to make the effort to put it in place.

Have a good long look at the Penny Cress and ask, "Am I taking care of myself right now and preparing for my glorious future?"

Like the story of this unique prairie plant, if we have financial intelligence and integrity early on, wealth will grow on our own money tree, and allow us to live the way we deserve.

# Prairie Sage

THE CLAY GROUND UNDER my feet is hard and cracked, and reminds me of walking on the old cement of a well-worn small town sidewalk. There is not even a hint of moisture to lend itself to the parched vegetation. Plants cling tenaciously to the ground, patiently waiting out yet another dry spell on the prairies. The unrelenting rays from the sun have bleached out the sumptuous foliage that came with spring, and replaced it with the soft, faded-green blooms of late summer.

I wonder how these plants can survive here, but I know Mother Nature has everything in hand. These plants grow here because over millions of years, they have adapted to this environment. They get everything they need to not only survive, but also to flourish. This is their land. This is where they belong.

The Prairie Sage is one such plant that makes its home here. The low, woody bush has many branches loaded with small, silvery, lance-shaped leaves. Blossoms are tiny, pale-ochre florets that cling along the stem. A wonderful aroma wafts up towards me, lifted into the air by the soothing west wind. In the fall, the brittle remains of this plant will break off at the base, and tumble and dance its way across the landscape on blustery days, just like in old western movies. The tumbling tumbleweed.

The Prairie Sage embodies the true spirit of the prairies. Unspoiled and free, this unique environment is expansive and genuine. Its soil is rich in nutrients, and helps support a wide range of wild plants and animals. Humans have settled here and turned the prairies into a patchwork of fields and pastures. Native grass has been plowed under to make way for barley, wheat, and other grain crops. Livestock graze in coulees and on open hillsides.

Things have changed dramatically on the prairies due to our influence. Small towns and farms now stand where great swaths of virgin prairie grasses once grew.

Growing food to feed the world is very important, and having land available to erect homes and businesses is the hallmark of an advancing civilization. But we must remain aware of how we impact our environment, not only here on the prairies, but also all around the globe. Nature exists in a delicate balance, and it does not take much to tip the scales.

We all depend on this planet. It is our home. But we have not always given enough thought to the beautiful environment in which we live. For too many years, we have taken what we wanted from nature, and simply dumped our waste in return. We have poured sewage into the water and pumped chemicals into the air without stopping to think about what we were doing, the damage we were creating, and the future impact we would have.

Although we cannot change what happened in the past, we can make better decisions about how we live on our planet today. We are smarter now, or at least we should be, and steps are being taken to halt and even reverse some of the damage we have caused.

When people saw what was happening to their beautiful world and the damage that was being done, they decided change was in order and collectively said, "That is enough." The groundswell of environmentalism has taken hold in every country, as reflected by the explosion of environmental organizations and initiatives. But as good as this changing tide is, there is still much more to do. The crusade towards environmental awareness is still in its infancy, and as with all things in their early stages, there are many growing pains.

As much as we would like to point fingers at big business or government corporations for polluting our environment, the truth is we are all responsible for the mess, and we must all contribute to the remedy. At times the problems seem overwhelming, and we ask ourselves, "What can one person do?"

We can make choices every day in our own lives about the impact we have on this land. We can choose not to litter, we can choose to recycle, we can choose to walk the two blocks to the store for milk instead of drive, and we can choose to upgrade our homes to being more energy efficient. These actions may not seem like much, but they will be noticed by others, and influence them to think about their own behaviors and the impact they have on the environment. Before long there will be entire communities, cities, and provinces working towards environmental change, with the ultimate goal of healing and protecting our natural world.

Let us look after Mother Nature the way she has provided for us. Let us respect what we have inherited and pass it along to the next generation in better condition than when it came to us.

Like the Prairie Sage, let us dance lightly across the landscape, and preserve it for future generations to enjoy.

# Goat's Beard

I have a Goat's Beard plant growing on the edge of my garden. My neighbors tell me to pull it up because it is just a weed, but I refuse to do so. I like the look of the Goat's Beard. It is a very tall, striking flower with a unique beauty all its own, and it deserves to have its place in the world respected. The fleeting blossoms look like pale-yellow sunbursts, with longer green spikes radiating from underneath. Slender grass-like leaves cling to a thick olive-colored stem, softening the long lines of the lanky plant.

The reason I am keeping this flower is in anticipation of the large, gauzy globe of seeds that will suddenly appear one late summer's morning, looking like soft grey powder puffs that will soon relinquish their seeds into the air. It is at this stage in its life when the beauty of the Goat's Beard really shines.

This plant teaches us that there is beauty and value at every age. So many times I have heard women lament the loss of their youth. They pile on creams, lotions, and hair dye in an effort to cling to a past image. And who can blame them? We live in a society that values all things shiny and new because companies have succeeded brilliantly in convincing us that newer is better. We must have those new clothes, cars, gadgets, and toys, but then we are encouraged to discard them and upgrade. And so it is sometimes with mature women.

Many societies in this world define beauty as something that exists only in youth. Indeed, the focus seems to be what's on the outside—soft and smooth skin, lustrous hair, and firm bodies. But like the blossom stage of the Goat's Beard, this external, youthful beauty is evanescent. It does not last and we all know it.

Society does not encourage us to see and value the incredible intrinsic beauty that exists in older women. As we march through time, that beauty, that unique, magnificent spirit we all have, remains constant and radiates outwards at every age when we are confident enough to allow it. However, too many of us are taught to only see the packaging. No question, the external packaging does hold some sway, but that is just one part of our divine being.

Is it not time to redefine what real beauty is, and to value the whole woman, inside as well as out? Do we not owe that to ourselves? And do our daughters and granddaughters not deserve to be seen as valuable at every stage of their lives?

The time has long passed for us to change our attitudes about what constitutes a valuable and beautiful woman. Aging does not have to mean decay and loss of physical attributes. A beautiful woman is one who shares her ageless qualities, such as being warm and endearing, gracious and charming, caring and compassionate, and wise beyond measure. She is a noble being who navigates through life with her head held high, and serves as a beacon for others to follow. The mature woman has an elegance of spirit, and a wisdom that can only come from experience. These are the qualities that make women beautiful, as well as valuable contributors to our society. Each of us already possesses these attributes in our heart and soul, and the time has come for us to focus our attention on these beautiful qualities, instead of just seeing the gift wrapping.

It is difficult to change the world's perceptions about growing older when we ourselves have deep-seated, negative beliefs about the effects of aging. We can be so quick to look at the down side—the sagging skin, loss of muscle tone, greying hair, aching joints. But even though some of these things do happen, we do not need to dwell on them. Our attitude about ourselves at our current age plays a huge role in how we continue down the road of life.

When we can approach each day with gratitude for what we have, and foster a genuine love for ourselves, everything we do and see will be framed within these affirming parameters. As we progress throughout our days, let us not focus on our aching bones or our upcoming doctor's appointments, but instead rejoice in the simple things—how good a deep, cleansing breath feels in our lungs, noticing the little flower poking its delicate head up from the ground, smiling anytime we hear children laugh while they play. These simple pleasures are in abundance and are around us all the time. The more we can draw our attention to them, the better we will feel during each minute of the day.

Another misguided perception about aging is that it is now too late to start anything. Many of us have convinced ourselves that we are too old to take dancing lessons, travel to Tibet, go back to school, or take up scuba diving. Actually the only thing stopping us is the limited boundaries we have put in place for ourselves. If we truly believe we are too old to learn how to ice skate, then we probably are. But why do we have these beliefs? Are they messages we have received from society? And if so, are those messages correct?

Instead, why not believe learning how to ice skate at seventy is doable? And why not take that trip to an exotic destination, or work towards a university degree, or go skydiving? When we become seniors, we do not check our hopes and dreams at the door. We will still have desires, and we will still have goals.

We need to be the change we want to see in our society. The mature woman must show the world, especially the youth looking up to her, that age is only a number, and she is just as vital and valuable as she ever was.

First and foremost, however, we need to believe in our own value. It is difficult to convince others when we do not entirely believe it ourselves.

Thankfully, things are beginning to change. More older women are embracing their age and celebrating the precious commodity that they are. They are remaining visible, and showing the world they are more vibrant and sophisticated than ever before. They have influence and power, enthusiasm and wisdom. Their beauty comes from a strength of spirit, an energetic force that let's everyone know the best is yet to come.

It is time to throw away our shallow and limited perceptions of what makes a woman valuable and beautiful. It is time to embrace the older women in our lives as they share their wisdom, warmth, and insights.

Let us all enjoy the blessings of having a Goat's Beard in our garden.

www.ingramcontent.com/pod-product-compliance
Lightning Source LLC
Chambersburg PA
CBHW050830160426
43192CB00010B/1966